FIFTY
STEPS
C L O S E R

FIFTY
STEPS
CLOSER

Group Counseling Guide in Reflections of
School-Aged Boys & Girls

Nicholas G. Minardi, Ph.D.

TATE PUBLISHING *& Enterprises*

Published by Tate Publishing & Enterprises, LLC
127 E. Trade Center Terrace | Mustang, Oklahoma 73064 USA
1.888.361.9473 | www.tatepublishing.com

Tate Publishing is committed to excellence in the publishing industry. The company reflects the philosophy established by the founders, based on Psalm 68:11,
"The Lord gave the word and great was the company of those who published it."

Book design copyright © 2007 by Tate Publishing, LLC. All rights reserved.
Cover design by Janae J. Glass
Interior design by Elizabeth A. Mason

Published in the United States of America

ISBN: 978-1-60247-891-6
1. Psychology: Developmental   2. Education & Training: Child
07.08.30

ACKNOWLEDGMENTS

I'm fortunate to have the family, friends, and inspirational figures I have and continue to discover in my life. Achievement in the absence of such fine companionship would be, without a doubt, an empty endeavor.

Inspiration comes from those who inspire us to be more than we could ever imagine on our own. For that I thank my family and childhood friends. I also give great thanks to my former high school coaches, John Georgeson and Mike Denney. Had my life not been graced by the experiences of encountering Professors Merlin Gramm, Lowell Rost, and Jon Klimo along the way, the conceptualization and evolution of this project would not have come about.

There is no way to calculate the overwhelming positive impact my friendships with the Scott Hall and Mike Torgerson families have had in my life. Their continuous support, over the span of many years, has been of great personal value. I am both honored and grateful to be considered their friend and in a heartfelt way...family.

Phyllis Scott, Barbara Shook, and Marti Reed have been three outstanding principals who gave me the opportunity to provide group counseling services for the students in their schools. I have greatly enjoyed being part of their educational support teams as well as a counselor for the students we served.

Finally, I would be remiss if I didn't acknowledge the influence of Maxwell and Bailey, my own two children, in the development of this project. They have been daily blessings and steady reminders of how precious, impressionable, and insightful all children are.

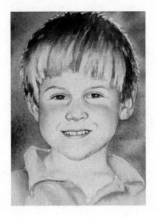 

A special thanks to the members of the Fifty Steps Closer project support team: Cherie Wharton, Shari Johnson, Julie Jamison, John Steffen, Marilyn Cochran, Bob Wiley, and Dr. Leo Marvin.

TABLE OF CONTENTS

PREFACE

Fifty Steps Closer is first and foremost a practical applications guide designed to help counselors, especially counselors who are new to the field, in conducting group counseling sessions with school-aged children. This manual is also intended to be a collection of fifty student reflections that recount the students' experiences of having participated in group counseling sessions.

The material within these pages attempts to weave together the process of conducting group counseling with the experience of the student in counseling. The rationale for combining the two features is as follows. When a counselor begins to understand how the student in counseling perceives what goes on in counseling, the counselor gains valuable insight. This insight can then be translated and refined to improve the counselor's effectiveness during the sessions and thus, in helping students. That is, when we as counselors begin to understand the perceptions and experiences of the student in counseling, we not only better understand the student; we help the student better understand himself.

A large majority of the lessons in *Fifty Steps Closer* has two components, the check-in phase and the activity phase. The check-in phase places emphasis on and explores family dynamics, interpersonal strengths and weaknesses, and school performance. The activity phase serves as a vehicle to help address relevant counseling issues that may either be at the core of the student's concerns or at least may touch upon areas in the student's life that are problematic. The counseling activities are designed to be fun, interesting, worthwhile, and allow the student to actively participate on multiple levels.

The reader will note standard similarities from one lesson to the next.

Every lesson begins with the "Lesson Name" followed by the "Goal of Activity." In this section, the counselor is provided a snapshot of what the lesson requirements are about. This section not only contains a brief synopsis of the objectives of the session but also information on, "Student Mix," "Size of Group," "Suggested Time," and "Required Materials" needed to conduct the group session.

The "Considerations" section of the lesson is a direct communication from the author to the reader. In this section, the reader will discover insights, obstacles, and concerns that the author thought noteworthy to share. In some lessons, variations on the activities are offered. This section was also put together in such a way as to encourage the reader to develop his or her own sense of delivery when conducting the activities without losing a general sense of direction.

By far, the heart of every lesson is found in the section entitled "Student Reflections." As you read this section, be mindful of not only what the student is interpreting, but also what the counselor may be trying to do. This section is often filled with insights and assorted clues not only about how students are interpreting what you're doing, but also what they're feeling, thinking, and trying to accomplish as well as avoid.

Readers will note throughout the book, this section represents more than just the re-telling of one student's experience in counseling. Rather, it is a personalized and meaningful account of how the sessions were experienced through the perceptions of fifty different students, one at a time. Keep in mind, however, that despite a multitude of similarities that may exist among group members, their recollections of those experiences have been filtered through a variety of attitudes, ages, abilities, and of course, issues.

With this perspective in mind, the reader may note that the author has taken at times, the occasional liberty of applying the benefits of acquired language to this section of text. Every attempt, however, has been made to keep the complexity of language and concepts as simple and true to the student's experience as possible. Not all terms or words used in this section are necessarily the words students have come to master. However, in the absence of words, what happens in counseling through the use of activities and insights, often allows the student to make those therapeutic connections, even though he or she may not have mastered the "right" words to describe his or her experience of the moment.

At the end of every lesson the reader will find a "colorable Backpack Supplement." The supplement is to be sent home with the student following each session. This supplement serves a dual purpose. First, it will serve as a reminder to the student of the counseling session (activity) he or she participated in and, ideally, the lesson learned. Secondly, the backpack supplement provides parents the opportunity to stay informed of the student's involvement in the counseling process. The supplement is generally informative as to the nature of the counseling activity yet void of specific content that might otherwise be considered confidential.

In formulating *Fifty Steps Closer* and in keeping with the counseling tradition, I believe the goal of the school counselor is to alleviate emotional discomfort and help the student adjust or re-adjust properly to the demands of daily living. This is in part done by moving the student to a place of insight, perspective, and when appropriate, behavioral change. I have come to believe, however, that the single greatest therapeutic mechanism of fueling change lies within the counselor's ability to instill within the student the unwavering belief that the counselor is someone who is personally invested and cares wholeheartedly about the student.

The activities presented in this book serve only to enhance the process of counseling and any intended lessons (therapeutic messages) are subject to change based on the flow of the counseling process. That is, consider the activity a ship and the counseling process the ocean on which the ship sails. The counselor is the captain and the group members are the crew. You begin with a map and if all goes well, you set sail, enjoy the trip, and arrive at the intended destination. The crew then departs, taking with them souvenirs and postcards as reminders of the journey.

Sometimes, however, the experience of the counseling voyage is dramatically different than the one outlined above. There has been occasion where simply getting the crew on board became the goal and in turn became an adventure unto itself.

Eventually, perhaps, the ship sets sail but you, as the captain, realize the intended destination will not be reached. Therefore, new goals are created as you attempt to salvage the voyage. Yes, there are lessons to be discovered, unexpected treasures if you will, whenever a counseling activity goes awry. Learning to recognize and utilize those unexpected treasures is, after all, what we as counselors are meant to do.

As a reminder to the reader, the lessons within are not detailed maps to be followed so as much they are a compass to help the counselor navigate the course of the counseling process with students of various ages and abilities. The reader should also be mindful that any predetermined lesson will not automatically take students to the desired therapeutic destination but with skillful guidance, just might bring them...*Fifty Steps Closer.*

"A SHIP IN THE HARBOR IS SAFE, BUT THAT'S NOT WHAT SHIPS ARE BUILT FOR."

~ William Shedd

GOALS AND OBJECTIVES

Goal of Activity: The counselor will introduce the student to the counseling group process, provide an explanation of the referral system, and the parameters of confidentiality. The counselor will further assist the student in establishing personal and academic goals for the current school year.

Student Mix: boys and girls of similar grade or age

Group Size: four to six students

Suggested Time: thirty minutes

Materials Required: index cards, pencils, permission slips, and treats

Considerations:

For most boys and girls, this will be the first session students participating in counseling will be exposed to. However, more times than not, most school counseling groups are open and ongoing. That is, boys and girls will come and go during the course of the school year. Thus, it is not uncommon for a student to join a counseling group that is already in progress and will have missed this introduction into counseling. The counselor may wish to consider meeting separately with any new group candidates and conduct this lesson before having those students placed in the ongoing counseling curriculum. The topics of confidentiality, safety, and goal setting will be a theme that runs throughout the course of counseling sessions. Students will certainly be at a disadvantage if they miss out on this springboard activity.

Students are referred to the school counselor primarily from parents and teachers for a wide variety of reasons. Regardless of who makes the referral, however, be sure to get a signed permission slip in your files as soon as possible.

I think that getting the student to buy into counseling is largely the shared responsibility of both the student and counselor. It's important that the counselor work hard at getting the student to want to participate in the counseling process. I've found that boys and girls who do not want to be in counseling have a way of undermining and sabotaging the process of counseling if made to attend. I strongly encourage counselors with limited group experience to initially omit including students who perceive that group counseling is yet just another form of "punishment." You may wish to consider having the resistant student attend group merely as an observer at first. You could also meet with the student individually, offering encouragement and support until a time comes when the student becomes more of an appropriate candidate for group counseling services.

The counselor can adjust this activity several different ways and still be able to meet the lesson's intent. Younger boys and girls are not always able to think in terms of goals and objectives. They are, however, able to imagine what they want to be when they are "grown-up." Having a student visualize, then draw a picture of him/herself as an adult, while you voice potential occupation and personal positive characteristics can be quite effective. From there, the counselor is able to chart some initial goals for that student. For example, if a boy sees himself as being a fireman as a grown-up, the counselor verbally retraces that path highlighting various educational, emotional, and physical landmarks that the student must obtain along the way.

Student Reflections:

My teacher had me meet our school counselor, Dr. Nick, today. He invited me to go with him along with some more boys and girls. We sat at a table in his office and he talked about maybe why we were there. Dr. Nick said we were invited to be in counseling maybe because our parents wanted us to be or maybe 'cause our teacher thought counseling would be helpful. He said maybe it might be for both reasons why.

Dr. Nick said even though our teacher or parent wanted us in counseling, we don't have to be here if we don't want to. I think what he was saying was that I can be in counseling if I want to be, but I don't have to be in counseling just because someone else says I have to be. I like feeling in charge, it makes me feel pretty important.

The counselor said that students who participate in counseling groups usually like counseling, have fun, and get along better with their families, teachers, and friends.

The counselor told us that there will be times when we may have to choose between going to counseling or doing other things like recess, music, and gym. I liked that he said we can choose if we want to go to counseling or something else. He said once we make our decision for the day we have to stick with it. I guess that meant that I couldn't go to music and then during music, change my mind just because I didn't like what I was doing.

Our counselor thought our first meeting should have three things to talk about today:

an introduction to say our name, grade, and teacher, talk a little bit about our family, friends, and school, and figure out what our school goals will be for the year as well as goals for things outside of school.

Dr. Nick gave everybody one of those little lined note cards and asked that we write down the names of our family members on one side and a couple of our goals on the other. I'm sure glad he was able to help me spell stuff. Some kids are worse spellers than I am. I figured that's why Dr. Nick wrote down their goals for them.

Like, we could have some goals about school stuff like getting smarter in spelling, reading more books, and not missing so many school days because of "sorta" being sick. We also got to make out goals for things like trying out for sport teams, making new friends, keeping old friends, and staying out of fights. Dr. Nick told us we could even make goals about family things, like planning big birthday parties for the people in our families, getting house chores done before we get killed, and learning how to not talk back so much.

Once all of that was done, the counselor collected all the cards. He read them to himself but asked questions if he didn't quite understand what had been written. A couple kids wanted the counselor to read the goal cards out loud, but Dr. Nick wouldn't do it. He said something about kids having personal or private goals. He also said he'd talk about personal goals later.

He told us that every now and then we're going to review our goal cards because he wants to see how close we're getting at reaching our goals.

Dr. Nick says that counseling group may last up to forty minutes some days and that our group will usually begin with check-in. Check-in is a time for us to talk about how our week went with family, school, and friends.

After check-in, the counselor will probably have a counseling activity. Dr. Nick thinks that counseling activities should be fun and interesting. He said they're also supposed to help us get along better at home, in school, and with our friends.

Dr. Nick spent some more time telling us about some of the activities we would be doing this year. Like he told us about how we'd be using stuff like bugs, batteries, and buckets of yuck! He really does make counseling sound like it's going to be a lot of fun!

The counselor then told us about privacy stuff. He said that lots of times kids talk about personal things during group and that we should not talk about another kid's personal stuff when we're not in group. The counselor said we can tell our parents about what we do in group but other than them, be careful about what we say to anybody else unless we have that kid's permission.

Some of the kids had questions about keeping things private or what Dr. Nick said was confidential. One boy had told us about his older brother wanting to run away from home and what the counselor at the other school did when he found out. Dr. Nick said something about how safety is his biggest priority, even bigger than keeping things private.

I think it was just about lunch time and Dr. Nick said we were almost about done. He gave everyone a piece of candy and said we all had done a good job for our first time in counseling group. He also told us he'd be back next week, and if we want to come back to counseling then we'd have to bring our permission slips back with us too. I left group eating my piece of candy thinking I was definitely going to come back.

Dear Parent,

Your child participated in our first counseling group today! In today's session we discussed how counseling works, how counseling can be helpful, and the rules involving confidentiality. We also developed a "map" to chart your child's academic, interpersonal, and personal goals for the school year. As the year progresses, look for your child to improve in those areas. Please contact the school counselor for updates or any concerns you may have regarding the progress of your child in counseling.

A TEAM

Goal of Activity: Using sport and the team concept, this activity is designed to highlight the similarities between family and team, identify positions or roles family members play, and promote unity within the family.

Student Mix: boys and girls of approximately the same age and grade

Group Size: four to six students

Suggested Time: thirty to forty minutes

Materials Required: assorted sports memorabilia including bobble-head doll, pennants, photographs, team blanket, colored pencils, multiple pre-cut paper bobble heads, popsicle sticks, glue, and Cracker Jacks

Considerations:

In this session the counselor should consider that not all boys and girls have experienced being part of a formalized team. Various degrees of explanation may need to be given to further explain the roles of "Most Valuable Player, Coaches, and Silent Stars." Most students, however, are aware of at least one football, baseball, or basketball team name. Writing the names of teams provided by the students on the whiteboard is helpful.

The use of visual aids such as pictures, posters, team emblems, and assorted team merchandise is always helpful in conducting this session. Many boys and girls will spontaneously report having similar memorabilia in their homes. The counselor should acknowledge each item, but be careful not to necessarily endorse the product in which the team emblem appears such as beer mugs, lighters, shot glasses, etc.

When transitioning from the team concept to the family concept, the counselor may consider using a sport's team picture as a bridge between the two concepts. For example, display a football team photo and ask the students not only about what position a particular player plays, but also ask, "Could this player also be someone's mom or dad?"

As the students begin to identify the members of his or her own family in the roles of MVP, Coach, and Silent Star, the counselor could reinforce the idea that under certain situations, roles can change. That is, the family's coach in one situation (dad, driving the car) may need to assume a different role (silent star) and take orders from the family's M.V.P. (mom with the map and perhaps a better sense of direction).

One variation on this activity with kindergarten and first grade students would be to eliminate the writing component completely. Start by verbally introducing the team concept, move to the family concept, and then spend most of the group time coloring the bobble-head cut-outs. While the students are coloring the figures, the counselor needs to verbalize the virtues of how important it is for families and teams to work together, define roles, and to learn how to celebrate daily victories.

Student Reflections:

My school counselor, Dr. Nick, invited me to participate in counseling group this afternoon. When I got to his office, I noticed lots of cool sports stuff all over his room. I saw pennants, posters, a team blanket, a seat cushion, a team thermos, and even a bobble-head doll. This was too awesome!

We started group with check-in and took turns talking about our week at home with family, at school, and with our friends. I didn't feel so much like saying much about myself or what's going on with my family. I wasn't sure if I should say how I was really feeling or if I should have just said everything is okay, just like the other kids do.

I get the feeling that the counselor would listen to me if I did tell him stuff. He looks interested in what the other kids say. I kind of like the way he looks at me and talks to me. He doesn't seem to be in a hurry and listens to what everyone has to talk about.

The last thing we did in check-in was to write the names of our favorite sports teams on the whiteboard. I had like five teams! Everyone got to write the names of at least three teams but nobody got more than five. After we did that, Dr. Nick got us started on the counseling activity.

The activity began with Dr. Nick asking for definitions of the words coach, M.V.P., and silent star. We decided that coaches are in charge of teams. Coaches are also supposed to motivate and get players to work hard. M.V.P. s are the most valuable players on a team. They not only get their job done like blocking or whatever, but they also help everyone else around them do better too. We figured the silent stars are the players who do what they're supposed to be doing without being noticed so much.

Dr. Nick then gave us time to talk about our favorite teams. For starters, we figured out that every team has a coach or a captain. Every team might also have a few M.V.P.'s, and every team might maybe have some silent stars too. Dr. Nick said that everyone on a team is important, and it takes everyone on the team doing their part to make the team a success.

Dr. Nick left group for a second and went over to his desk. He said he wanted to show us a picture of his favorite team, his family! They weren't even wearing the same uniforms! He introduced us to the coaches of his family, the M.V.P.'s of his family, and the silent stars of his family. Dr. Nick then told us that families and teams are like two sides of the same coin, like that you can't have one without the other. I liked that he showed us a coin. He said, "Heads can be your family and tails is your team."

He asked us to think of our families as a team. Who are the coaches? Who are the most valuable players? Who are the silent stars? In my family, my dad is definitely the coach, but I think my mom owns the team because of the way she bosses him around.

Dr. Nick then gave each of us some blank pieces of paper cutouts in the shape of a person's head. He told us to draw the faces of our families coaches, most valuable players, and silent stars, one face on each paper cut-out. I got to tell Dr. Nick that I'm one of my family's silent stars. That means I don't complain about everything like my sister does.

I really liked this part of what we were doing. Even though I'm not so good at drawing, I like using color pencils. When we were done, the counselor gave everyone a popsicle stick to go along with each of their bobble-head cutouts. We used glue to stick the heads to the sticks.

Dr. Nick said that every family needs to have team goals rules for personal behavior, bedtimes, something to look forward to, and consequences for team members who don't follow the rules. Even though we're on a team, Dr. Nick said we won't ever be traded to another family so we should always do our very best no matter what role we have as a member of our family team.

When I was leaving his office after group was over, Dr. Nick gave me a small box of Cracker Jacks to share with my family and told me something about always rooting for the home team.

Dear Parent,

Your child participated in a counseling group today with the school counselor. The activity presented today dealt with the similarities between families and teams. Your child was encouraged to think in terms of the various roles family members play as well as the responsibilities each have in helping to make the family more successful. Be sure to ask your child about whom he or she identified as your family's Coaches, M.V.P.'s, and Silent Stars! You might just be surprised!

THE JUGGLER

Goal of Activity: To improve student self-esteem and confidence while instilling the belief that the student can learn how to deal more effectively with the multiple demands of daily living.

Student Mix: boys and girls of approximately the same age and grade

Group Size: four to six students

Suggested Time: thirty to forty minutes

Materials Required: box of soft plastic balls and sticky labels

Considerations:

Most students enjoy this activity very much. Having a box of multi-colored play balls is really important for the success of this activity. Everyone will want to pick his or her own color balls; yet if the counselor wants to help minimize a controversy or potential protest, he or she should remind the boys and girls, "You get what you get and you don't throw a fit!" All the boys and girls know by now or will quickly learn that phrase.

The counselor should spend a few minutes preparing the counseling room before the group arrives. The removal of the table and any other fragile or dangerous items would be a good idea. If the weather is nice and the wind is not too much of a factor, take the group outside in a safe and secure area.

During check-in be sure to emphasize the things that compete for the student's time. For example, the counselor may say something like, "Sounds like you have a lot to do at home between homework, feeding the animals, and other chores." Another worthwhile phrase to use might be something like, "Wow, if I had to do everything you have to do, I'd have to be three people!" A statement like this helps to make the student feel good about who he or she is and also conveys to the student a sense of respect. Be sure to keep track of what things compete for each student's time. Consider writing them down on a sticker as the student shares them during check-in.

Counselors need not necessarily know how to juggle in order to teach this lesson. Just being able to throw the ball up with one hand and catch it with your other hand is usually enough to get by. Remember, all you have to do is sound like you know what you're doing.

Keep in mind that teaching a student to juggle is not an easy task. Don't spend all day focusing on mastering this skill. Most boys and girls are going to have a one or two ball limit. Start everyone out with just one ball and take turns allowing everyone to juggle. Avoid having everyone juggle at the same time.

Students in kindergarten through second grade generally don't have great motor skill coordination. Just getting the ball from one hand to the other will be enough of a challenge. For the younger boys and girls, one ball will be all they'll need but let them try two balls for sure. It will make them feel as if they're really juggling!

You will encounter some boys and girls in secondary and middle school who really have a talent for juggling. These kids are a lot of fun to watch and you may want to showcase them in front of the other group members. One variation you may consider, have everyone take turns being in the showcase. Have the "audience" (the other members of counseling group) chant along with the juggler the things in his or her life that compete for time. This chanting effect has a way of getting everyone involved, pulling for one another, and sends a message to the juggler that people are supportive of his or her efforts in being successful.

Be sure to re-emphasize the importance of concentrating, effort, and practice, practice, and more practice. Allow everyone to take home two juggling balls to practice with during the week. It has been my experience that nearly everyone in group will want and possibly demand more balls than they can handle. Be sure to praise them on their desire to become overachievers, yet allow the student to earn another ball the following week if he or she comes back to group and demonstrates improved juggling skills.

Student Reflections:

Today was my day to be in counseling group. The counselor called my classroom, and our teacher answered the phone. My teacher seemed really glad to be hearing from Dr. Nick!

When I got to the counselor's office, I noticed the table was gone, but our chairs were still there. Dr. Nick told us to form a circle with our chairs and sit down. As we sat there, most of the kids in our group started swinging their legs back and forth. The counselor said, "Knock it off," because someone might get hurt and that would mean two people would be sent to the office. I think I knew what he meant by that.

Group started with check-in. Dr. Nick wanted a volunteer to go first to talk about family, school, and friends. He also wanted that person to name two things they do that takes up lots of time. Those things might be homework and chores or even sports and music. He volunteered me to go first. I didn't mind going first because after I told everyone about my week, I could pick the person who would talk next.

After everybody had checked in and said the things they do that take up lots of their time, Dr. Nick said he was going to teach us how to juggle! He told everyone that understanding how juggling works is easy, the harder, really more challenging, part is actually doing the juggling!

Dr. Nick had a big box of soft plastic balls that looked like the ones from a play land I've been in at McDonalds. He gave everyone just one ball and showed us what to do. He said there are three things we must remember: toss the ball up, catch the ball with our opposite hand, and switch the ball back to the tossing hand.

We got to practice for a little bit. One ball was pretty easy, but some kids can't catch. I picked up this other kid's ball and was going to show everyone I could juggle with two balls, but the counselor told me that maybe I could do that later.

While we juggled, I heard some kids say, "I can't," or "This is too hard," but Dr. Nick encouraged everyone to keep at it.

After a few minutes of juggling practice, Dr. Nick stuck labels on the balls we were using. The labels had words on them, like homework, chores, mom, dad, gymnastics, football, job, family, brother, sister, and play.

Dr. Nick then gave each of us a second ball to juggle that also had a word on it, just like the first word but different. My two words were football and homework. Dr. Nick said these are the things I told him about earlier that compete for my time and concentration.

Now the counselor had us take turns juggling two balls! For most kids in our group juggling wasn't too easy, but this one kid was doing really a great job! I wasn't as good as the best kid was, but I sure was having a lot of fun!

While we were taking turns juggling, we were told to say out loud the two things we need to work on at juggling during our day. Like I said, for me it is football and homework. For some kids it's like going between Mom and Dad's house, for this one boy it was homework and chores. Olivia said she needed four balls because of her parents' divorce, homework, babysitting, and sports!

It was kind of funny hearing everyone talking out loud to themselves and trying to concentrate on juggling at the same time! I dropped my ball a couple times, but each time I did the counselor told me to keep trying and also told me I was getting better at juggling. I liked hearing that I was doing good, it made me feel great even though I wasn't an expert juggler just yet.

For about ten minutes everyone worked on getting better at juggling, but this one girl threw one of her balls at another kid in group. Dr. Nick saw her throw the ball and asked her about it. I think she lied. Dr. Nick told her that for right now juggling two balls was too much for her to handle. The counselor picked up the ball that the girl had thrown and read the word that had been written on it. The word was "step mom." He then asked that girl how she feels about her step mom, but the girl just got madder and didn't answer his question. I heard Dr. Nick ask her if she would maybe talk to him later about getting her ball back. She said she would.

As we were finishing group, Dr. Nick said we could keep the balls we used today to take home and practice our juggling skills. He reminded us that even though juggling is easy to understand, learning to juggle is really hard because it takes lots of effort, concentration, and practice for a long time. The counselor said he really wants us to become better jugglers because it would be good for us and it might even help our parents with their juggling too.

Dear Parent,

Your child attended a group counseling session that focused on the development of skills required to become successful in "juggling" busy schedules. Students were given the opportunity to identify a few of their responsibilities including chores, homework, and athletic obligations. Good News! When given enough time to practice and plenty of encouragement, your child appears quite capable of learning how to manage multiple tasks!

RECYCLING MYSELF

Goal of Activity: To help students learn to differentiate between the effects and consequences of productive and non-productive goal-seeking behaviors.

Student Mix: boys and girls of approximately the same age and grade

Group Size: four to six students

Suggested Time: twenty-five to thirty-five minutes

Materials Required: pencils and paper

Considerations:

This is a pretty good activity. I found it works better with secondary students than primary grade boys and girls. There is a fairly strong writing component involved in this activity, and it also challenges students to think abstractly. As in any writing activity, boys and girls are often challenged by spelling. That is, many students are concerned about their spelling abilities and may feel inhibited to write freely. Be sure to remind the students that the activity is not about writing correctly as much as it is about having relevant behaviors in mind.

The concept of recycling may be new to some students and still a fuzzy process for others. You may want to have a picture of the neighborhood recycling station and review exactly how recycling centers work. Having examples of recyclable materials on hand and what they can be transformed into is a good idea. Be sure to emphasize that many recyclable materials were at one time, helpful and appropriate. However, as time goes by, some things that were useful are no longer functional and fail to serve their initial intention. You may tell kids for example, "Crying to get what you wanted as a baby may have worked pretty well for a few years. Now, crying to get what you want only makes you sound like a complainer, and all that will do is make things worse."

One variation I have found to be successful is to use the whiteboard rather than individualized pencil and paper. In using the whiteboard, the counselor is the only one who does the writing. This not only saves time, but it also lowers the amount of anxiety some boys and girls feel when it comes to pencil/paper activities. In using the whiteboard, I feel that it's very important the counselor continue to spend as much time with the group as possible. That is, as in most groups, the counselor participates as a member of the group with the students. As you begin to formulate your own philosophy about group dynamics, be aware and curious to any therapeutic differences that may exist between teaching a group and being part of the group.

Student Reflections:

Today, Dr. Nick came by our classroom and took me to be in counseling group with those other kids again. Group started off with us telling about ourselves by saying our name, age, and grade. The counselor then asked us to say something important about our family, school, and friendships. This is what he calls doing check-in. He also said that this is how we will usually start our groups. I don't think I like this part so much.

During check-in, Dr. Nick asked everyone to think about something a friend or family member does that bothers us. Like, something we don't always agree with. For example, chewing food with their mouth open, "butting" into a private conversation, or taking stuff that doesn't belong to them. Everyone was pretty quick to come up with lots of things that make us mad!

The counselor then asked us to invent a substitute or replacement behavior for the one thing that person does that we think is annoying. Like, for the one kid whose brother chews food with his mouth open, Dr. Nick said maybe he could just start chewing with his mouth closed or use a straw for some stuff.

That worked out pretty good. It was fun thinking about how we could just get someone to stop doing annoying things by having them do something else or that one thing differently. I told that kid he should get his brother to eat in a different room or maybe even over at the neighbor's house.

After everyone had taken their turn at check-in, Dr. Nick got us ready for the counseling activity. We were given a sheet of paper and asked to fold it down the middle "hot dog bun style." Across the top of the page we were told to write the word materials. On the top of the left-hand side we wrote the word "steel." Then on the top of the right-hand side we were told to write the word "plastic." I hate all this writing!

Once all that writing was done, the counselor told us to write the names of old household and school junky things made of the same stuff we had listed on our papers. On my paper I wrote down the words bent paper clips and broken ruler. I put the paper clips under the heading steel and my broken ruler in the plastics part. We had like three minutes to write the names of as many junky things as we could think of from our homes and classrooms.

Dr. Nick asked if any of these things could be recycled, like turned into something that might become useful and helpful to us again. Lots of kids gave some pretty good ideas! For example, old nails could be recycled into new cans and old plastic containers could be changed into new plastic cups.

We were then asked to turn our papers over and write the word behavior across the top of the page. In the left side column, we had to write down stuff what kids do that aren't helpful in trying to get what they want. Like, Dr. Nick asked that we think of things we've done in the past to get something we wanted maybe like throw a fit. Instead of getting what we wanted, all we really ended up getting was in trouble for not getting what we wanted the right way.

The girl sitting across from me remembered when she kept "nagging" her mom for candy at the store. This one boy told about the time he "borrowed" money from his father's change drawer without asking for it.

After everyone talked about the stuff they've tried that didn't work, our list didn't look so good. It had words written on it like whining, stealing, complaining, denying, blaming, and pouting on it. Dr. Nick let me put a star by my favorite one.

On the right side column, we were asked to recycle each of those non-helpful behaviors into ones that would actually be helpful in getting us what we want. The counselor called on everyone to think of a memory we had when we were able to get something we wanted by acting or behaving in a more better way.

This one kid who says he's living in a group house for boys told how he was able to get more privileges by completing more chores and making his grades higher at school. Another kid told a story about the time his parents gave him a chance to ask for just one thing under twenty dollars in the toy store. If he asked for more than one thing, he would get nothing. Well, as hard as I bet that was, the kid kept himself from driving his parents' wacko and only asked for one toy. He got it too!

After we finished trading crappy and useless ways to get the stuff we wanted with better working ways to get that stuff, our list started looking a lot better. We had things like working hard, being polite, using good words, taking turns, being responsible, and staying organized written down. Dr. Nick told me I could put a new star by my favorite one on this list then erase the old one I had from the other part. He told me this new one of working hard will work way better than the old one of whining.

Dr. Nick gave everybody who worked hard in counseling group a brand new piece of candy. For a couple kids who didn't work very hard, he offered them a piece of recycled candy. It looked like it was kinda re-wrapped. He said the recycled candy was still probably pretty good and none of it had ever been chewed, maybe licked, but definitely not chewed. I think I'm pretty sure he was just kidding.

As we were getting our stuff together to leave group, the counselor said that everyone, even our parents, might want to think about recycling their old non-working, crappy behaviors into more positive ones. He also said we should notice our own behaviors at home, in school, and with our friends and be sure to recycle our old worthless behaviors for better, more helpful ones.

Dear Parent,

Today in counseling group during check-in, students had the opportunity to talk about family, school, and friendships. The counseling activity focused on your child learning how to identify and recycle his or her old ineffective behaviors into new productive behaviors. For example, "throwing a fit" was recycled into "staying calm and talking it over." Be sure to ask your child about his or her "old study habits."

BOP IT, PULL IT, TWIST IT

Goal of Activity: The student will be encouraged to learn to follow a set of directives in a timely manner.

Student Mix: boys and girls of similar motor skill abilities

Group Size: six to eight students

Suggested Time: forty-five minutes

Materials Required: Bop it, school map, and treats

Considerations:

This activity is designed to address a common characteristic that many boys and girls share who participate in the counseling process; they don't follow directions.

I think it important that the counselor build an appropriate foundation for the activity and this can be done during check-in. Encouraging the student to think before speaking (action) and then to make a reasonable decision (one candy now or two later) actually has helped students perform better in this activity.

This is a very straight forward lesson. Listening and following directions is a skill to be learned. Learning if or when to question directions will be an equally important lesson for each student to learn in time.

Be sure to have students take turns in this activity, otherwise some boys and girls will lose interest and become a distraction for the kids who are trying to follow directions. Learning to focus and follow directions is after all what the activity is all about.

One variation on this activity I have implemented with older boys and girls is to request that they write down a list of directions they typically receive. The directions may come from parents, adult relatives, and teachers. The student must also be able to explain why each direction may be important. Once the list is completed, the numbers of directions are tallied. The student is then given the Bop it and challenged to complete an equal number of Bop it directions.

Student Reflections:

Today I went to counseling group with our school counselor, Dr. Nick. Like last week, we began the counseling session with check-in. Dr. Nick wanted everyone to say something pretty important about family, school, and friends. We also went over each of our own goals. Dr. Nick said important could be pretty much about anything that made us happy, sad, or whatever.

One of my goals was to get in less trouble with my teacher. My teacher always tells me to pay attention and to listen better. So far this week, I only got detention one time and that was for not listening to directions during a test. I was really doing pretty good!

During check-in the counselor gave us the direction to think before we speak. He told us he would be keeping count of the number of times each person said: "Um, Ah, or Uh." The person with the fewest "non-thinking" sounds would get to go first in the activity today.

Dr. Nick was just getting ready to give everyone a piece of candy after check-in, but then he gave us the choice of having one piece of candy now or waiting until we were done with group and maybe getting two pieces if we were good listeners. I thought I should take my candy now before something went wrong.

Once everyone else told Dr. Nick what they were going to do about the candy, we got to start the counseling activity.

Dr. Nick started by writing the word directions on the whiteboard. He asked for a definition of the word. Everyone gave an answer, but we got it kinda broken down to mean that directions are words that instruct the reader or listener to do something specific. For example, parents use words that instruct their kids to clean their rooms, take out the trash, and don't make any messes. Teachers also use directions that tell kids to sit quietly, be patient, and come to school on time, being ready and prepared to learn.

Dr. Nick then told us we would be doing an activity today that involved following directions. I didn't think I'd be liking this activity very much, but he also said the directions wouldn't be very complicated or too hard. In fact, he said the directions would be so simple that anyone could follow them if they were fast enough.

I got really excited when Dr. Nick pulled a Bop it out of his sack! Everybody knows what a Bop it is! The Bop it runs on batteries and when it's turned on, gives directions to the person who's holding it. The more directions you follow, the faster the directions start to happen. The directions tell the listener to "Bop, Pull, or Twist" different parts of it before you get zinged with a sound that means you took too long to follow the direction.

It was so cool when the counselor told us we would be using the Bop it in our counseling activity today! He said we were going to have a contest and the person who follows the most directions without making any mistakes would be the champion. I asked him, "What will I get when I win?" He told me, "In less trouble." I didn't get it.

Snap! He started the activity with the person who had the

fewest number of "non-thinking" sounds from check-in! This meant I would be going last! Man, I really wanted to go first, but Dr. Nick reminded me I needed to follow directions.

We took turns following the directions the Bop it told us to do. Everyone counted out loud the number of times in a row each person could reach before getting zinged with a buzzer sound.

Dr. Nick kept track of our totals and we played until everybody had like three or four turns. One girl reached twenty-five straight directions before missing and ended up with a total score of fifty-three! I got up to like seven straight before getting zinged, but I kept getting better the more I played. I yelled out one time that this stupid thing was broken, but I don't think that Dr. Nick heard that.

When all that was done we had to sit around the table and talk about the activity. Dr. Nick says that following directions can sometimes be a lot of fun, just like it was today. He also said that learning to follow directions can save a person's life. For example, Dr. Nick asked us the following questions:

1. What are three directions you would give someone traveling alone?

2. When is a person most likely to stop, drop, and roll?

3. If you're ever feeling frightened and home alone, what are three good directions to keep in mind?

4. Name three directions your mother has told you to follow if you're at the mall and can't find each other?

5. Name three directions your teacher wants you to follow if your school campus has a lock down?

We talked about these questions and some more questions too. Dr. Nick makes it sound like following directions is pretty important and I guess maybe sometime they are.

Dr. Nick says sometimes we won't always understand the why behind the direction, and even if we do understand, we might not care. However, not caring or not feeling like following a direction isn't a good enough reason not to do it. He said following directions might one day save our life or someone else's. Like he said for example, maybe my dad might see a car coming at me on the street and yells at me to get out of the way! Dr. Nick said that I could always ask my dad why later but only if I followed his direction now.

The counselor said that kids get lots of directions every day from parents, teachers, and coaches telling us to do a whole bunch of stuff. Dr. Nick wants us to keep in mind that those directions come from people who not only care about us, but they also know what's good for us even though we don't always understand why or even think they're right.

On the whiteboard, Dr. Nick wrote something about trusting and believing in the people who see us every day. He said that following directions is a cool way to show those people we respect them. He also said it's a neat way to find out how much discipline we have in ourselves.

Leaving the counselor's office today, Dr. Nick gave everyone a school map with directions to go to the principal's office. Once we got there, the principal gave everyone a certificate that read: "Remember, if you want to make your way in life and be successful, safe, and smart, then learn how to follow directions."

On my way out of the principal's office with my award and treat for having done a great job, I was thinking that I'm not usually sent here because I follow directions so good. This is a way better feeling than the one I usually have when I leave here! This is a great feeling!

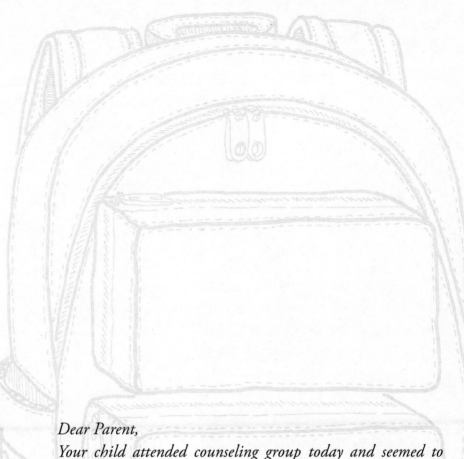

Dear Parent,

Your child attended counseling group today and seemed to have had a great time! The counseling activity focused primarily on improving your child's ability to follow directions within a reasonable amount of time. Specifically discussed were following directions at home with chores and in school with assignments. What made the activity so fun, however, was our use of the "Bop it," toy. Everyone showed a ton of enthusiasm and ability in being able to follow directions!

STRESSFUL EVENTS

Goal of Activity: To promote awareness and dialogue of common stressful situations students are frequently challenged with. The student will also identify symptoms of stress and learn how to improve his or her stress management abilities.

Student Mix: boys and girls of similar age and grade

Group Size: three to four students

Suggested Time: thirty to forty minutes

Materials Required: twenty-four index cards and two types of treats

Considerations:

This is a very easy activity to pull together. The activity is designed to encourage students to share information about stressful times in their lives under the guise of a game. The counselor not only has the opportunity to inquire about how stressful events were handled but can also facilitate a discussion regarding effective versus ineffective ways of dealing with stress.

This lesson can be introduced several different ways. It doesn't always need to be competitive in nature, especially with the younger students.

However, older students seem to enjoy friendly and supportive competition with one another. In this case, the counselor also plays the role of judge in helping to determine how well each student answered the stress-related questions. I think it's beneficial to require the older, more verbal kids to work harder for their matching pairs of cards.

Be sure you have enough table and or floor space to spread out the matching cards. Also, try to discourage kids from spontaneously rearranging the cards on their own. Some kids will attempt to manipulate the game in order to secure more cards than their peers. Often, this may be interpreted as a form of cheating and may have something to do with the student's placement in counseling group.

No matter how the lesson unfolds, it's very important to identify the symptoms of stress and for each boy and girl to walk away from the counseling session with one or two effective ways of dealing with stress-related symptoms.

Student Reflections:

Dr. Nick called me to his office for counseling group today. He seemed pretty darn happy to see me. He smiled, gave me what he calls lucky knucks (which is kind of like shaking my hand but we just each make a fist and lightly put our knuckles together,) and asked how I was and if my day had been going pretty good. Some more kids joined us before we actually got our group going.

We got started with check-in. Each of us had been told to say something important about our family, school, and friends. Dr. Nick told us we could ask any member of our group one question about the family stuff that kid had talked about during check-in. The counselor reminded us to be respectful of one another's personal information too. He said we shouldn't be telling other people outside the group what's going on in another kid's life unless that kid tells us we can.

This one girl told how she overheard her parents talking about buying Christmas presents for the kids in her family. Well, everyone in our group knows this girl has a younger sister who's at our school. The counselor explained that, without permission, nobody should be telling the younger sister or anyone else what gifts the parents have bought. Dr. Nick said that it would for sure ruin the surprise and it would also be breaking one of our rules about keeping things private because that's no one else's business.

Now I understood what he meant about keeping stuff said in group...in group!

After check-in, Dr. Nick spent some time with us talking about how we're making progress on our goals.

Our counseling activity for the day started when Dr. Nick asked if any of us knew how to play a memory game using matching cards. Sure! Everyone in our group had played that game before. The counselor showed us the cards we would use for today's matching game. The cards had either a symbol or a word written on them. There were like twelve pairs of cards, twenty-four cards total, I think.

The signs or words on the cards were all about things like: money, homelessness, moving, school trouble, divorce, unemployment, being scared, drugs and alcohol, illness, death, and jail.

The cards were turned face down on the table. We took turns trying to find two cards that matched. If like for example, we flipped a moving card over and then flipped a matching moving card over, we could keep that pair of cards only if we could tell of a time we could talk about a move we had done. Dr. Nick also asked like how different people in our families handled being stressed out about those things.

The first set of cards I matched was actually about moving. I told how our family moved when I was in second grade. I remembered having to say goodbye to my friends and how sad I felt. I also remembered how nervous I was on my first day in the new school. I felt everyone was staring at me, and I also thought I wouldn't have anyone to hang out with at break or lunch.

The counselor then asked how my parents handled the move. I think he forgot that it's just my mom, brother, and sister living at home with me. My dad lives in another house. I just looked at him and said, "I told you before my dad lives somewhere else!" He said he forgot and he said he was sorry because he knew that's not what I wanted.

Anyway, I told Dr. Nick that my mom was excited about moving. She told us that my brother and I would be sharing one room and my sister would be getting her own room! We would also have more money for groceries and could even get cable television!

I think though that my mom was also a little worried about moving so far away from my grandma. I had heard her crying one night on the telephone while she was talking with my grandma. I told my mom on the way to school the next day that everything was going to be fine and Grandma could come visit us sometimes.

During the game as we played, we kept track of the cards. When there were no more cards to match, the game was over. At the end of the game everyone counted the pairs of cards they had. No matter how many or how few cards we had, the counselor gave everyone a piece of candy and said we all won because we're all winners!

Dr. Nick said he wanted to talk about the cards we played with. He said all the cards we used could cause some people to feel stress. He said stress starts out as a signal inside our brain like a light that flashes on and off going "beep-beep-beep." He said it lets us know something is changing. Feeling anxious, angry, sad, scared, or worried could be what the beeping noise is all about. He also said that this feeling may work its way into our stomachs caus-ing a pain, give us headaches, and even mess up our appetites and how well we sleep.

I was glad that we got to play the game again. This time when we played, we also had to come up with a better way to deal with each of the change cards. Like, this one kid said that playing catch, talking about it, riding a bike, or roller-skating might be good ways to deal with the stress of changing schools. Talking to a friend, counselor, or a nice uncle who doesn't drink beer were other things kids said would help deal with being stressed.

Dr. Nick said that it's important to learn how to handle stress in good ways because handling stress in bad ways can cause more stress! Bad ways of handling stress could be like using drugs or alcohol, skipping school, and stealing stuff.

When we were all done, Dr. Nick gave everyone the choice of candies and hoped that having to choose between a chocolate crunchy and a chewy fruity wouldn't create too much stress in our lives. He said we could talk about that next week if it did.

Dear Parents,

Earlier today your child attended a counseling session with several other boys and girls. The activity in counseling group centered on how boys and girls can learn to recognize and then deal appropriately with stress. A card matching game was used to facilitate recollections and a discussion surrounding potentially stressful situations. Ask your child about the group activity and see if he or she can describe some methods for dealing effectively with the symptoms of stress.

OVERCOMING OBSTACLES

Goal of Activity: This activity is designed to encourage and reward persistence and creativity as the student learns to identify and overcome obstacles in obtaining goals.

Student Mix: boys and girls of similar age and grade

Group Size: four to six students

Suggested time: twenty to thirty minutes

Materials Required: paper maze with various built-in obstacles such as dragons, rivers, walls, quicksand, mountains, fire, etc. A sticky notepad and encouragement stickers (Good Job, Well Done, Awesome, Terrific Work) is also required

Considerations:

Filing cabinets, boxes, and desks can be placed between the students and their chairs at the onset of group to provide them with the experience of being successful in overcoming obstacles. This sets the right tone for the activity and offers the student proof that he/she can overcome obstacles. This proof may be offered during the session in the form of reassurance. For example, the counselor may say, "Everyone here today has already demonstrated super ability in overcoming lots of obstacles in just getting here to group." For many students, aside from the obvious built-in room deterrents, those obstacles might include going to bed on time, getting up on time, and of course, arriving to school on time.

During the second half of the activity after a mental connection has been made between the paper maze obstacles and real life obstacles, it is important to encourage students to discuss some of the obstacles they have already faced during their lives in reaching their goals. This is a time when the counselor can really reinforce and build a student's confidence.

One slight variation on this activity would be to have students create their own list of obstacles to overcome in obtaining their goals. Instead of having a maze filled with ready-made dragons and quicksand, the maze could be prepared with blank areas. Students could then fill the blank areas with obstacles of their choice. When the maze is complete and the point in overcoming obstacles has been made, allowing the student to color his or her maze often increases the possibility that the maze will make it home with the student and be displayed in a place of honor, like on the refrigerator or a bedroom wall!

Student Reflection:

Dr. Nick called me right on time for counseling group today. Of course, anytime I'm called seems to be the right time. When I got into his office, I saw my name printed on a card taped to one of the chairs. I was thinking that was probably the chair I should be sitting in.

The only real problem I had getting to my chair was that I had to go around some stuff to get to where I was supposed to be! There were boxes, desks, and even a filing cabinet in my way. I got there though and once everybody got to their chairs, we were ready to start group.

Group started off with check-in. This is when we get to talk about how our week went at school, with friends, and at home. Dr. Nick tried to get everyone to say as much as we wanted to about what's going on, but he also wanted us not to use up other people's patience.

The counselor also asked if our teachers said anything kind or encouraging to us this week. I was surprised to hear what some of the responses were! One boy told us his teacher said he was super spontaneous when it came to sharing his answers out loud with the other boys and girls in class. That sounded pretty good!

Dr. Nick started our activity by giving everybody a sheet of paper with a maze on it, but before we could start doing the maze, he showed us several pretty tricky areas. There were dragons, fire pits, stone walls, quicksand, barbed wire, aliens, rivers, deserts, and even an ice mountain. He said we could go around, up, over, underneath, or try and go through those things if we wanted to. He also said we could either get points or lose points at each obstacle, depending on what our choice was for getting past those things. Each spot had a place to write down whatever our answers were.

Like, Dr. Nick said he was going to keep track of our choices of how we dealt with whatever was in our way. It looked like he had an answer sheet or something with points on it that he could use to help figure out if our answers were any good or not.

Everybody got a pencil and the maze only took a couple of minutes to finish. When everybody got done, we got to take turns and say our answers out loud so everyone could hear them. Dr. Nick scored our maze choices and gave points for things like good thinking, creativity, and being smart. He took away points for answers that had unbelievable, wild, and crazy parts to them. Like, climbing over a wall was worth ten points. Waiting for a comet to destroy the wall received zero points.

I think I did pretty good. This one kid always tried to hammer everything. He didn't get a very good score. Dr. Nick told him not everything that gets in his way can be hammered. He said sometimes you might just have to leave things alone, go around stuff, or even pour some sugar on it and sweeten it up a bit.

One thing he said that I didn't get was something about figuring out how to use one obstacle to help get past another one. Like he said, "Climbing to the top of a mountain now to get a really good look at all the other stuff that might be in the way one day." Uh...like whatever that meant.

Our counselor told us that just like in a maze, we all have lots of obstacles too. "Today's dragon," says Dr. Nick, "might be tomorrow's parents getting a divorce."

For each obstacle in the maze, the counselor had a real life obstacle that he told us about. Like, the river was really about not having any electricity. The ice mountain was really about not being able to make friends. Another thing was really about being held back a grade.

I began to understand what the counselor was getting at when he placed stickers over the obstacles on my maze. He covered up the maze obstacles with real word stickers. Some of the stickers read: "No Electricity," "No Friends," "Not good in math," and "Held Back!" Now I got it!

We started to talk about other challenges we might have to get past someday. Things like problems in school with subjects and grades, being bullied, moving to a new home, changes in our families, people getting sick or dying, and what to do if a parent goes to jail.

Dr. Nick said that when we get older, we'll be having some of the same obstacles our parents and grandparents have too. Things like mountains of bills to pay! He said if we can learn to do good math now, then one day taking care of our money stuff may be less of a challenge. What he said earlier now made sense! He also said we might have to learn how to keep a job we don't like, and we'll still have to deal with oceans of laundry and yards of weeds! That sounds just like my mom!

The counselor asked us to raise our hand if we wanted to talk about any old obstacles we got past or any obstacles that we're working at getting past right now. Several kids had stuff to say. One girl, who I know for a fact isn't any good in math, told how she got past that by asking for extra help from her teacher at lunch time. The boy sitting across from me talked about fighting his feelings of liking his step mom too much. When he was asked about what he meant by liking his step mom too much, he said that he wants only to like his real mom and thinks the only way to do that would be by not liking his step mom so much.

Dr. Nick told the kid he pretty much understood what he was talking about but he also wanted to meet with the boy by himself to talk about getting past that obstacle in a good way and still be loyal to his mom. The counselor wanted all of us to use our family, teachers, and friends to help figure out the best or "least" worse ways in getting past some of our harder obstacles.

As we left Dr. Nick's office, everyone was given a sticker that had the words "Be smart, never give up, and never surrender" written on them.

Dear Parent,

In counseling activity today your child faced a variety of obstacles. Dragons, fire pits, and mountains were a few of the obstacles the kids in group had to overcome. During the activity those obstacles were transformed into real life obstacles such as divorce, parental incarceration, death, relocation, and financial hardships. The students then shared some of the personal obstacles they've overcome. Your child was encouraged to be creative, energetic, and to never give up in overcoming future obstacles.

TWISTER

Goal of Activity: To help the student understand that lying, stealing, and cheating not only compromises his or her integrity, but it also leaves the student in a very uncomfortable position with family, teachers, and friends.

Student Mix: students of similar age; gender mixing not advised

Group Size: three to four students

Suggested Time: twenty to thirty minutes

Materials Required: Twister game

Considerations:

Elementary-aged boys and girls seem to have fun with this activity. It requires some physical movement, a little coordination, and a reasonable amount of space to play. The counselor could consider placing tumbling mats under the Twister playing surface. Some students in counseling fail to use good judgment as they attempt to carryout the commands of the game. Showing off becomes their first priority, and thus the students may become prone to injuring themselves or others.

Depending upon the number of players and the size of the students involved, you may want to limit the number of players on the playing surface. Think about having all boy or all girl groups. I've noticed older boys become more curious about the girls they see in skirts and dresses stretching from one point to another than they are at learning the value of the lesson at hand. It's an understandable distraction but one that will quickly undermine the goal of the activity.

If time permits, you may wish to spend additional time at the end of group processing the students' past or current experiences of telling lies to keep their promises in tact. Try not to be too surprised by what you hear, take notes, and be prepared to investigate some issues further.

Student Reflection:

Dr. Nick invited me to attend group counseling today! There were several kids in our group. We told about ourselves by saying our names, age, grade, and our favorite food. We were also encouraged to say something important about our family, school, and our friendships.

As I was sitting there, the counselor showed us a question he had written on the whiteboard. The question was: "Have you ever had to tell a lie in order to keep a promise?" Charles, one of the kids in our group, told how his friend invited him to a sleep over on Friday night but he had to promise not to tell anyone else. One of Charles other friends, Kyle, who was not going to be invited to the sleep over, asked Charles if he knew anything about a sleep over one of their friends was having on Friday. Charles told him no.

Dr. Nick said that was a perfect example of being asked not to tell the truth in order to keep a promise. Several other kids in group gave some more examples. Once everybody said what they wanted to say, we got to start the counseling activity.

The counselor surprised me when he told us that we would be playing a game called Twister! I already knew about the game because I've played the game before and I've also seen the game on television commercials.

The rules were simple: two people could play at once and we all got to take turns being on the mat. The object of the game was to do what you were told without losing your balance by like sitting or falling. The directions were pretty easy, too. Things like, "Right foot yellow, left hand green, right hand blue, and left foot red," were examples of the directions we needed to follow.

After everyone had got to play the game, we sat down off the mat and Dr. Nick asked if we knew what an uncomfortable position was. Heck yeah! He just had us all tied up in knots! Dr. Nick said he wanted us to think of the words difficult or uncomfortable in a different way.

As we were sitting there, I leaned over and told my friend that I saw Melinda's underwear. We started laughing and then he tried to look too. Dr. Nick didn't notice us laughing.

Again, the counselor asked everybody if we've ever been asked to lie, steal, cheat, or to keep the truth from another person. I looked around at everybody to see if they were going to raise their hands. I wasn't going to raise my hand unless somebody else did first! It was kind of funny because everybody was looking around at each other!

Dr. Nick said that sometimes the people we know as family members, friends, and even strangers might ask us to do something we feel is wrong, like by lying, stealing, or cheating. By agreeing to do the wrong thing, we help put ourselves in a very tough spot. The counselor reminded us of the question he had asked us during check-in. It was the one about telling a lie in order to keep a promise. When he said, "So, what does that question have to do with what we're doing in this activity?" Then I began to understand what he meant by uncomfortable positions!

We got to play the game again, but now the directions had

been changed. Dr. Nick only let boys go with boys and girls go with girls. He also said something about being kind and respectful or not getting to play.

Dr. Nick called out statements like: "Just lied to your mother, left hand green, cheated your uncle in monopoly, right foot blue, kept your aunt's change from the grocery store without permission, left hand red, made a promise not to tell who took the teachers answer book and lied to the principal about it, left foot yellow."

His statements were kind of funny but also pretty real too. I could definitely see and feel what the counselor meant about getting into uncomfortable positions if we were to lie, cheat, or steal, especially if we make promises that mean doing something wrong.

When we were done playing the game, Dr. Nick told us to think really hard about the choices we make because we're going to be responsible for them. We were asked to remember that uncomfortable positions, like in Twister, are fun in games but not so much fun with our teachers, family, and friends.

Dear Parent,

Your child attended a counseling group today with the school counselor. Students participated in a game of "Twister" which placed all of the kids in some very awkward positions! The counselor then helped students make the connection between "Telling Lies" and "Awkward Positions." The boys and girls in group shared with one another their own experiences of placing themselves in awkward positions. The group also talked about avoiding awkward positions by simply telling the straight truth.

THE PRIVATE
INVESTIGATOR

Goal of Activity: The student will be encouraged to grasp a greater understanding of the word attributes. More importantly, the student will be supported and rewarded in his or her search for discovering positive attributes in him/her self and others.

Student Mix: boys and girls of similar age and grade

Group Size: three to four students

Suggested Time: twenty to thirty-five minutes

Materials Required: magnifying glasses, small paper sacks, quality crayons, and treats

Considerations:

Counselors should be somewhat mindful that vocabulary plays a large role in this activity. You don't want to get caught up spending too much time defining words. Select quality words that students may already know and introduce just a few new words. Keep in mind that it is a good idea to have duplicate quality crayons for the students to find. That is, it's okay to have several for example, kind crayons. I find it easier for most boys and girls to share stories of kindness rather than rack their brains for examples of courage in their friendships. Remember, the younger the kids, the simpler the words.

Depending upon how much time you have with your students in group that day, try to spend some time getting them thinking about how, when, and with whom they plan on implementing any of these positive attributes into their friendships. Getting the kids to rehearse or role-play future positive behavior is of tremendous value. For example, use the whiteboard to keep track of the student's family and friends. As a group, brainstorm ways to display or convey qualities such as kindness, sincerity, and forgiveness. In a group format boys and girls often feel less inhibited to participate due to the verbalized support of their peers.

Student Reflection:

Dr. Nick came to our school today and called me to go to group. I waited sorta, pretty good until we got more kids to come. While I was waiting, I wanted to look around in his cabinets and storage boxes trying to find any toys or other neat stuff. It didn't hurt my feelings too much when he told me to please keep my curiosity to myself. It would have hurt my feelings if he had said that in a stricter or meaner way the way my uncle does like, "Get out of there! What do you think you're doing?" I wasn't embarrassed or anything, but I sure knew what he wanted me to do. Well, maybe I was a little embarrassed.

The counselor started counseling group by checking-in with everyone about their week with family, school, and friends. Today Dr. Nick really wanted us to concentrate on our friendships. He asked us if any of our friends needed our help over the past week and in what ways we were able to be a friend to them. Everyone had something to say. Some kids just kept talking. I was glad when the counselor helped those guys just get on with it. He told this one kid that he needed to make his point right now and to stop taking other people's time.

On the whiteboard, Dr. Nick wrote some words that describe a good friend. Good listener, patient, understanding, respectful, considerate, generous, and loyal were some of the words he wrote. Everyone in our group agreed those words describe the qualities of a good friend.

When we finally got around to starting the activity, Dr. Nick asked if any of us knew what a private investigator was. Sure! Everybody seemed to know. The counselor wrote down our answers and kinda put them all together. He said a private investigator is a person that pretty much looks for people or things that have been lost, misplaced, or stolen.

It was fun when he asked if we knew of any books, movies, or television shows that had private investigators in them. Everybody started talking at once! This one girl said how her Aunt Cherie has a poster of some guy named Magnum in her bedroom. She said her aunt calls him a hunky stud and would marry him if her Uncle Robert didn't find out about it. Of all the answers given, I think Scooby-Doo was my favorite, even though there were lots of good ones to choose from.

I was really surprised and pretty excited when Dr. Nick told us we were going to be private investigators today! He said he needed us to find some really important crayons that had either been misplaced or lost in his office. He called those missing crayons "quality crayons."

Each of us was given a magnifying glass and a little sack and then told to begin our search for the missing stuff! Even though he told us we could begin looking, I didn't really know for sure what I was supposed to be looking for. I don't think nobody did.

Dr. Nick had to tell us the whole thing about quality crayons. He said that pretty much everybody has crayons that aren't so much different than the kind that come in those big yellow boxes with rows and rows of different colors. He also told us that sometimes people lose site of or can't find their crayons. That's true what he said. Everybody I know has crayons, and I know I've lost some of mine too. All of us said we know crayons can get lost, misplaced, and even forgotten about until they can be found.

When Dr. Nick explained that quality crayons are really just crayons that have positive words written on them that describe something about a person. I kinda knew what he was talking about, especially when he showed us some crayons he had. These crayons had some of the words we used on the whiteboard taped to them.

The counselor then added some more positive words to the list he had on the whiteboard. He added words like honest, courageous, hopeful, truthful, promise keeper, and encourager to the list of those friendship qualities. Then he told us that all of the words listed on the whiteboard were taped to a whole bunch of crayons hidden all over the place in this one part of his office for us to find!

On his signal, we began our search for the missing positive quality crayons! After just a couple minutes of looking over, around, above, and behind stuff, the counselor called a stop to the hunt. We sat back around the table to show each other the crayons we'd found.

For every crayon we had, Dr. Nick asked that we try and remember a time when we were that way with our friends. For example, the girl who found the crayon with the word considerate on it, told about the time she let her friend take cuts in front of her in the lunch line. She also gave her some money for food because she knew the girl didn't have her own money and was hungry. Everyone in our group talked about it and agreed that was very considerate and thoughtful!

If we found a crayon with a quality word that we couldn't think of any examples, we could give an example of how we could be that way in the future with our friend. That was just like when

Tyler had found the word hopeful. He said that if any of his buddies' moms get sick, he would say a whole bunch of prayers for her. Dr. Nick told Tyler that not only would his prayers be hopeful, but they would also be kind and compassionate too. I didn't know what that last word meant, but I liked that Dr. Nick said it had something to do with a gift from the heart.

Dr. Nick even told us about how sometimes people can have crayons and qualities like hope, feeling safe, trust, and self-respect stolen from them! He said stuff like that can be ruined by other people if we're not careful. He told everybody in a really serious voice that we should talk to a counselor if we ever feel like someone is trespassing and stealing our right to feel safe, happy, and good about ourselves.

I pretty much heard what was being said, but the kid next to me gave me a shove and told me I was spacing off. I looked up and everyone was staring at me. I felt embarrassed. Dr. Nick asked me where my thoughts were at, but I didn't really want to say out loud. I was thinking about...something.

In group today, Dr. Nick had us looking all over the place, like under chairs and tables just like real private investigators to find quality crayons that describe people. Dr. Nick reminded us that everybody pretty much has quality crayons somewhere. Maybe though, they've been lost, over looked, or just forgotten about and not used for a real long time. He said when we get back to class and then later on home, that we should help our friends and family find their quality crayons too!

Dr. Nick let everybody keep each of the quality crayons we'd found along with some candy I found in his cabinet. As the other kids left group, I sorta stayed behind until I was the last one there. I waited and didn't say much but I was feeling pretty sad about something Dr. Nick said in group. Dr. Nick asked me to stay with him for a little bit and go over some of the crayons I had found. He said we could start by putting them in order of being important and then figure out which ones my family or friends might be breaking.

Dear Parent,

Your child participated in a counseling group today with several other boys and girls. The theme of the counseling activity focused on "becoming a private detective." The counselor recruited your child to conduct a search in his office to uncover valuable attributes. Your child searched for "Quality Crayons" colored with honesty, kindness, respect, loyalty, etc. Students were then given the assignment to find those "lost" attributes in their family members, classmates, and friends.

STAR SEARCH

Goal of Activity: To provide the student with the opportunity to consider his/her life in terms of a pattern. In using this pattern perspective, boys and girls may be able to see themselves and their lives more clearly. The counselor will also encourage and empower the student to take more of an active role in determining the pattern of his or her life.

Student Mix: boys and girls of similar age and grade

Group Size: four to six students

Suggested Time: thirty to forty minutes

Materials Required: star paper, pencils, glow in the dark star stickers, and colored pencils

Considerations:

As in most groups, I prefer to insert a clue during check-in as to what the activity will be about. It's not necessary for every counselor to do that, but I like planting the idea early and coming back around to it at group's end. Students will offer a variety of answers to the question: "Does yesterday have anything to do with today or tomorrow?" Try to find one that lends itself toward the activity and move on from there.

The star chart really needs to be nothing more than a photocopied piece of 8.5x11 paper with twenty to thirty star shapes scattered about. Use a marking pen to make the shapes of stars. As a counselor, you might find it interesting to simply examine the pattern each student creates. I think it worthwhile to consider these patterns to be somewhat diagnostic in nature. Be curious if you encounter a student's pattern that goes from one end of the paper to the other end in what appears to be scribble fashion.

Boys and girls intuitively have a sense for and communicate in one way or another if they have lived a life full of abrupt transitions. They may not be able to verbalize their experiences, but they will act them out. To some extent, that just may be part of the reason that these students are in counseling.

With kindergarten and first graders, I've eliminated the question regarding yesterday, today, and tomorrow. Time remains a very abstract and illusive concept and most kids that age still have difficulty telling time, let alone understanding enough about time to process it beyond thoughts of right now. For those boys and girls who have not reached an ability to understand or process time very effectively, consider providing them the star chart with the assignment of drawing a line from one star to the next. You will be able to talk them through the rest of the activity.

Providing crayons or colored pencils for the younger kids to use and engaging them in conversation about what was going on in their lives while they work on their star chart has been beneficial. You will notice that most boys and girls will talk quite freely while their hands are busy.

Student Reflection:

The counselor called me to counseling group today with some other kids from school. We had to spend the first part of our group doing check-in. Dr. Nick, the counselor, always wants me to talk about my family, school, and friendships. It seemed like he wanted to know how I felt about everybody and everything! He even wanted to know how old I am! I don't really like to talk about stuff all the time. Sometimes, I just want to do the activity.

I tried to get by with just saying, "Everything is fine." That didn't work so good. He made me say at least three things that are going on at home, in school, and with my friends.

After we were finally done doing check-in that lasted forever, Dr. Nick asked everybody: "Does yesterday have anything to do with today or tomorrow?" I guess we all talked about that and Dr. Nick helped us figure out if those three days had anything to do with each other. I didn't get it. One girl said, "I went to bed last night, woke up this morning, and I plan on staying awake until tomorrow." I thought it was a very good answer! Dr. Nick smiled and said her answer was very smart. He also said it was time to get ready for the counseling activity.

The counselor gave everybody a piece of paper that had like twenty stars all over it. We were told to put our pencil point next to any of the stars on the paper as our starting point. He then told us to write our birth date along with the number one next to that star. He showed us how.

You could get however many stars you wanted because of your age. So, if you were like nine years old, you could get nine stars to connect. Dr. Nick said we were supposed to connect the stars by drawing a line from one star to another. You could only use any star just one time. Each star we connected would be given a number in order. Like you start with number one, draw a line to another star, which would be number two, and do this all the way up to your right now age.

Once everybody did this, we got to hold up our papers for everybody to see. Nobody had the exact same picture and everybody's paper was very different looking! Two pictures looked pretty neat, almost like stars in the sky. This other kid's paper looked liked she had just scribbled from one star to some different star way across her paper! It looked like one of those things that measure earthquakes or a fat guy's heartbeat!

Dr. Nick told us we're all different and even though we might have lots of stuff in common, no two of us are exactly alike, not even our star charts.

Dr. Nick talked to each of us and asked us to try and remember something about each age of our life. For example, some of his questions he asked were:

What school did we attend?

Where did we live?

Who did we live with?

What were the names of our friends?

What was going on in our life at that time?

How did we make it from one year to the next?

We wasted like a whole bunch of time talking about everybody's growing up. I don't think Dr. Nick seemed to mind that some of us were drawing on our papers as the other kids talked. Maybe that's why he had colored pencils sitting out.

The counselor told us that with each star we add to our charts as time goes by, we could create a pretty neat pattern. He also said it would be important that each of us try to make sense of our connections from one star to the next.

Like in this one example, Katrina told about how her family moved into her grandparent's house after her mom died and from there she started a new school. This one fat kid in our group, who said he lives in a foster house, talked about moving from one family to another because no one wanted him.

Dr. Nick told Chubby to hold his star paper at arms' length away from his chest. He said that from a distance, he could look at all of those different houses or placements as having something to do with his choice of behaviors instead of holding it so close to his heart and thinking no one loved him.

The counselor told us that just like yesterday, today, and tomorrow, it's going to be important to figure out not only where we've been but also how we got there if we want to make good choices about where we want to be in the future.

Dr. Nick asked the kid who repeated the third grade, "Why do you think you were held back last year?" The boy said his teacher didn't like him, his parents wanted him to stay back, and the school would not let him go to the next grade. I thought the kid had some pretty good answers. I know I don't learn very well from teachers I don't like either. Dr. Nick said he understood what the kid was talkin' about and agreed a little bit and that there could be some truth in everything the kid said. When Dr. Nick asked that kid if it was okay to look at his report cards from last year, the kid said, "Okay." Well, that kid had like a whole lot of F's that year for his grades. He also had lots of teacher comments that said he didn't do very much homework, studying for tests, or any school projects.

Dr. Nick pointed out that when it comes to looking at all the stuff that led us to where we are right now, we also have to think about what we did or didn't do too. Sometimes, what we did or didn't do yesterday, not only changes today, but maybe changes what happens tomorrow too.

I guess that seemed to make sense. I told that kid who failed that's it's kinda like me not getting ready for dinner on time. Like if I mess that up and I don't get to eat dinner now, then I'll be starving later. Dr. Nick just looked at me and told me I was amazing!

As we were getting ready to leave counseling, Dr. Nick gave all of us a glow in the dark star sticker. He told us to take it home along with the star chart we had worked on in group. He said we can choose any place we want on our star chart to put our next star. That place could be on the honor roll, in college, or somewhere in pro sports! He also said that bright stars keep us heading in the right direction even if it's really dark out and we sometimes feel like we're lost and kinda scared. He said everybody has to make choices that help get us to our next stars.

I noticed that on the back of my star chart Dr. Nick had written, "Star by star, today will turn into yesterday and tomorrow will be here before you know it."

Group was pretty good today, and I didn't even have to say too much.

Dear Parent,

Your child did a great job in counseling group today! All the boys and girls were encouraged to participate in check-in. We also did an activity using a star chart. The activity was designed to help boys and girls better understand how past decisions/behavior effects current and future directions. For example, how not studying for a math test yesterday, will affect their test score today and math class placement tomorrow. Much of what we do can be seen in terms of behavioral patterns!

ROCK AND SAND

Goal of the Activity: To help the student identify some of the strengths and weaknesses of significant family members and friends. The student will also develop a broader understanding of the discrepancy that often exists between his or her unfulfilled expectations and the abilities of significant others.

Student Mix: boys and girls of similar age and grade

Group Size: four to six students

Suggested Time: thirty to forty minutes

Materials Required: sand, polished rocks, and small containers

Considerations:

Before doing this activity, think about how the kids in your group will respond to having sand. Normally, sand will get all over the table and floor. Kids are also known to throw sand or accidentally knock the sand bucket over. I'm sure the school's custodial staff would appreciate it if you did this activity outside or vacuum your office area after group is completed. Doing this activity on a table covered with a plastic table cloth works pretty well too.

Analogies don't always translate easily for most kids, especially the younger children. Work hard at the translation, but don't be surprised if you feel you have to answer most of your own questions. Be patient, kids will understand the activity on some level. They are very tuned into the physical differences between rocks and sand. Kids don't always have a good grasp of their feelings or how their feelings come to be. They can, however, tell the differences between a big rock and a bucket of sand. In part, your objective in this activity is to plant the seed of awareness, which eventually the student will be able to draw upon.

Spend some time with the older, intermediate-aged kids going over their expectations for the important people in their lives. As you can imagine, disappointment in another person is often the result of the expectations we have created for that particular person. Don't be surprised, however, to hear how much these kids have been disappointed by various family members. Hear what the kid says, be sympathetic, supportive, and when appropriate, encourage the student to see sand as tiny bits of individual rocks. That is, try to help the students adjust their expectations and find the positive qualities of the important people in their lives, no matter how small they might be.

Student Reflection:

I went to counseling group today with some other boys and girls. When we got to the counselor's office, Dr. Nick told us again about some of the reasons why he likes that kids get to be in counseling group.

Counseling can be fun

The counseling activities are interesting

What we do in counseling will help us be more successful at home, in school, and with our friends

During check-in today, the counselor went over each person's goal cards, the ones we filled out at our first group meeting. I was surprised that he also had a copy of everybody's school progress reports. Now he knew everything about everybody! He even had comments from our teachers on those reports about our effort, behavior, and grades.

When it was my turn to do check-in, I talked about one of my family goals I had been working on. The goal I have for my family is to spend more time together. Every Sunday night I unplug the television and bring out a bunch of board games for our family to play with. If the weather is nice, I go into our garage and get stuff for us to play with like bats, balls, and gloves. Sometimes, I find a Frisbee or something my dad likes to play called trackball. So far, so good, I think everyone in my family likes the games and activities we play and our time doing stuff together.

At the end of check-in, Dr. Nick wanted to know who our best friends are and to tell him why that person is our best friend. He also wanted us to name somebody in our family that we really look up to and tell why. I told about my dad and how good he's been doing since he's come home from this one place called rehab.

The counselor called on everybody to hear their answers. He wrote down the names of our best friends and the names of the people in our families on the whiteboard. After all that stuff got done, it looked like we were going to finally get to do an activity.

Our counselor put a big old rock and a bucket of sand on our table. He said he had just got back from the beach and wanted to show some us some stuff he got.

We all had the chance to put our hand in the bucket of sand and to touch the rock he had brought. It wasn't great or any-thing, but it was kind of cool and lots better than reading class. He then wanted us to think about ideas on how the rock and sand were both kinda the same and kinda different.

This was actually pretty hard to do, but he kept telling all of us we could do it. One kid said that sand is soft and rocks are very hard. Another girl said that you can throw sand at a teacher's car and not get into as much trouble as throwing a rock at a car.

Dr. Nick had started writing most of our answers on the other side of the whiteboard across from the names of our friends and family members he had written earlier. Not every answer made the list, especially the one girl's answer about throwing at cars.

This next part was even harder than the first part! We were asked to think of times when the sand might be better than the rock. Like, sand is better to walk barefoot on at the beach than rocks are, but rocks are better for climbing on than sand. I thought that was a pretty good answer. Lots of kids gave good answers. I liked the one about having sand in your eye more than having a rock in your eye.

Dr. Nick then wanted us to figure out how the way we described rocks might be like some of the ways we think about the people he had written on the whiteboard. I had no idea what he was talking about. It helped that he gave an example. He said, "Ben's dad and Darian's mom are very much like a rock because they are sturdy and have been strong for a long time. These are also people that Ben and Darian can count on not to break or crumble when they are needed the most." That helped me to kind of know what he meant.

I also liked that Dr. Nick drew lines from the words we used to describe rocks to the people we like and look up to. He said that one of the reasons that maybe we like and admire the people we do is because they are sturdy, solid, and always stay the same, just like rocks! Dr. Nick said we can call a person like that "Rocky."

We also had to talk about sand and figure out why sand might be like people we know that didn't make our list. Dr. Nick said that some people might wash away at the first sign of trouble. I said maybe there are some people who mess with my life and make me grouchy, just like when sand gets into my underwear! Everybody laughed when I said that!

This kid named Jacob didn't laugh. He said how his real mom is sometimes like sand. He told us that even though his mom can be nice and soft, she also makes him cry when she starts drinking and yelling about stuff. He said that it's sort of like when you get sand in your eyes. Dr. Nick said we can name people like that "Sandy."

Dr. Nick asked if anyone could describe someone who is both like rock and sand. One boy said he could count on his dad for some things like money and clothes but not for the other things like keeping promises and doing stuff together. I think some kids in our group were listening because I saw them shake their heads up and down.

Dr. Nick asked me if my dad had disappointed or let me down lately. I told him sometimes. The counselor asked me if I would tell him about what sometimes means. I told him that on Sunday my dad took some of me and my mom's money to buy some "weeds." Dr. Nick told me he knows how much I love my dad and that my dad's actions don't always live up to how much I love him. I wanted to talk about something different then so I went over to the candy bowl and started talking about candies I like. Dr. Nick said I could stop back at lunchtime and choose any one I wanted to.

Toward the end of group, the counselor asked us to remember that both rocks and sand can be alike but also different. Both have good things about them and not so good things about them, but lots of times it just depends on what we're expecting them to be. Dr. Nick kinda looked at me and said that sometimes we all want somebody who's important to us to be just a little bit more bigger and stronger than they already are and it's really disappointing when they're not. I'm not sure what that meant but I felt for sure like it meant something.

Leaving counseling group today, Dr. Nick gave everyone, except that one girl, a special polished rock and a tiny, little bag of sand to keep as a reminder of what we did in counseling.

Dear Parent,

Your child attended a counseling group today. Group began with check-in and we discussed family, school, and friends. The counseling activity compared the qualities of rocks to sand. We took those individual, yet over lapping qualities and applied them to people we know. Some people are like rocks; consistent and dependable. Other people are like sand; they may wash away when we need them the most. Be curious if your child uses the names "Rocky and Sandy" to describe folks they know.

TOWER OF POWER

Goal of Activity: To encourage and promote family unity through the identification of activities that lead to building stronger families. Students will also become aware of factors associated with family collapse.

Student Mix: boys and girls of approximately the same age and grade

Group Size: four to six students

Suggested Time: thirty-five to forty-five minutes

Materials Required: stacking blocks, family activities list, horns, noise makers, and peanut butter log treats

Considerations:

Students enjoy this activity. Not only does this activity work well for identifying traits of building a successful family, it also lends itself toward team building.

It's a good idea to keep students away from the table on which the structure is being built. That is, consider having the table on one side of the room and all the chairs with the students seated in them away from the table. Too often a student will accidentally or sometimes intentionally shake, bump, or push up against the table if they are seated too close. When this does happen, any notion you had of improving group unity secondary to identifying factors that improve family cohesiveness, has been lost.

If time becomes an issue due to assemblies, fire drills, award ceremonies, etc., you may find yourself falling behind your group schedule. Consider calling together a monster group. That is, pull together two groups of kids close to the same age if possible. For sure you will want to have a second container of building blocks. Have one big group or split the groups up into teams. You could also save time without losing effectiveness by providing students with a mix of suggestion and blank cards. Suggestion cards provide clear and direct ideas for students to implement with their families. The blank cards allow boys and girls the opportunity to create their own ways of increasing family unity. Either way, it's going to be an adventure for everyone involved including the counselor! Running a monster group will be a gentle reminder to the counselor as to why he or she did not want to become a classroom teacher or has left teaching to become a counselor (smile)!

Student Reflection:

I was invited to be in counseling group today with our school counselor. When everybody came in and sat down, Dr. Nick told us we all did a good job getting here without anyone getting run over, knocked out, or killed.

Group began with check-in. Just like last week, Dr. Nick said he really wanted everybody to say something pretty important about families, school, and friendships. Some kids tried not to say more than, "Everything is fine," but Dr. Nick didn't let them. He kept on them, especially when it came time to talking about family stuff. He asked everyone the same question, "If you could be any member of your family other than yourself, who would you be and why?"

When it was my turn to do check-in and to answer that question, I said I'd be my cousin. I told Dr. Nick I'd be my cousin because my cousin has all this neat stuff and he goes on vacations at the same time with his mom and dad.

Once everybody did check-in, I knew it was time for the counseling activity.

Dr. Nick brought out a box of wooden logs about three or four inches long. I knew what they were because I've played with them lots of times. They're building logs! I've got these at home and so does my cousin.

The counselor gave everybody like nine logs each. He said we were going to build a tower by taking turns answering just one question. The question was, "Can you name something that helps to build a family?"

Whenever it was your turn to give an answer, everybody else in the group decided if your answer was good enough. Dr. Nick said that good enough just has to sound reasonable. So like if your answer was good enough, you could add your log to the stack. If it wasn't good enough, then you couldn't add your log to the tower and would just miss your turn until the next time around.

Dr. Nick pointed to each member of the group and asked for an example of a reasonable or pretty good answer. Eating together, playing games, doing yard work, and going shopping together were some good ones.

Not good enough answers were things like having three different TVs on at the same time with people in different rooms, reading by themselves, and everyone walking around with their own set of headphones on.

Dr. Nick kept track of all the answers by writing them on the whiteboard. The game would be over after everybody with a good answer used their logs. Like I said, if your answer wasn't so good, you didn't get to use that log to help build the tower.

It took a little while to build the tower, but it was fun for sure. When we got done building the tower, we got to celebrate with horns and party makers! Dr. Nick also gave everyone a prize. He even gave me a smarty piece of candy!

We only celebrated for a little while before all that changed. The counselor had this one kid who didn't use up all of his logs become the tower wrecker! Dr. Nick said logs could be taken away from the tower one at a time for every answer that could make a family fall apart.

The kid who the counselor had picked was William. Dr. Nick told him that he could begin taking away a log from the tower with every "bad" answer he gave, only if everyone else in our group agreed his answers were really, really bad. But the thing was that William couldn't take logs off the top of the tower, he had to take them from the bottom part!

Well, it only took William to say like three bad things before the tower fell down. The first thing he said was lighting your house on fire. The next thing William said was hitting your step mom in the head with a shoe while she was sleeping. The last thing he said was sneaking beer into the house and drinking it in your brother's room. Everybody pretty much agreed his three things were pretty bad.

I saw Dr. Nick put William's name on a blue ribbon he had at his desk. He told him to stop back to his office at lunch time today so he could give it to him and maybe talk some more about our activity.

Even though William had said some pretty bad answers, everybody wanted to start talking about bad stuff too! It seemed like everyone had something to say about an uncle, aunt, sister, brother, mom, or dad who messed things up with their family.

Michelle said how her cousin messed up her family by selling drugs at school. A kid next to me, named Franklin, said that his grandpa had to go to jail for messing up at the daycare his mom was in charge of. I saw Dr. Nick write Franklin's name on a ribbon too.

The counselor had us read aloud all of our good answers written on the whiteboard. He told us he wants us to practice, practice, and practice all of those good things. He also gave me a list of all those family building ideas to take home for my family.

We could only leave group if we could remember one good thing from our list without looking at it about how to build our families "Tower of Power." Dr. Nick gave everybody a peanut butter log treat if they could answer that question with a good answer.

Dear Parent,

The counseling activity your child participated in today involved the use of stacking logs. The logs were used as a means of helping boys and girls understand how to go about "building" stronger families. The students also became aware of factors that could even make the strongest of family structures come tumbling down. Please be sure to ask your child to name three positive ways to help build a stronger family as well as some things to avoid.

THE POWER OF
PERCEPTION

Goal of Activity: To help students become aware of the discrepancies and inconsistencies that often exist between the actual mood and facial expressions of another person. The student will also be encouraged to practice the appropriate methods of expressing his or her feelings and how to politely investigate the feelings of significant others.

Student Mix: boys and girls of similar age and grade

Group Size: four to six students

Suggested Time: twenty-five to thirty-five minutes

Materials Required: facial expressions poster, mirror, and index cards

Considerations:

I like to keep the size of this group to four students. Six works, but I think you can get a lot more accomplished with four. I obtained the poster for this activity at a local teacher supply store. In the absence of finding a poster that displays various expressions of emotion, search various kid magazines, or better yet, create your own using people from the school.

This is really a good activity for allowing the student to offer personal information freely. This activity allows the counselor the chance to simply enjoy listening to what the boys and girls have to share about themselves. This activity requires very little effort on our part to direct, and you may be surprised how much you enjoy just going along for the ride with the kids on this one!

You may also discover that the use of a mirror really gets the kids into the spirit and joy of this activity. Before you use the mirror, make sure that the student has identified and verbalized the emotional memory he or she was asked to retrieve. Otherwise, kids will only want to make faces and be silly. I'm not saying that's a bad thing but as a counselor, we must be mindful during our fun and silliness of the underlying responsibility we have in creating the opportunity for insight and understanding to unfold before each and every student.

Student Reflection:

I was in the principal's office when Dr. Nick came looking for me today. I hate it when I get in trouble for other people making me mad and hitting them! I went with him to his office and he called for a couple more boys and girls. I pretty much knew everybody in group, even this one kid who made me hit him yesterday out at the bus line.

On the whiteboard, Dr. Nick showed us what he had written: "I ask questions and listen because I care about you." I asked if that had anything to do with our activity. He said he would talk about that later, but he also said he liked that I was curious.

For introductions we were asked to say our name, age, grade, and whose classroom we're from. It sounded like most of us were fifth graders because I knew most of the fifth grade teachers from last year when I was in fifth grade. After we got through that, we started check-in.

During check-in, we talked about how we thought our week went with our friends, at school, and with our families. The counselor thinks that school, family, and friends are really important parts of our lives. He says that if we pay attention to those things we learn to take better care of ourselves.

Dr. Nick wanted us to describe two memories we've had at home, in school, or with friends that was a good and not-so-good memory. He said a good memory at home might be like remembering the time your dad taught you how to ride a bike. For most kids that's a good memory because you feel happy and excited. A not-so-good memory at home might be something like burning your hand on the stove. It's a not-so-good memory because you got burned, and you were probably feeling angry and maybe embarrassed because you were told to be careful in the first place.

My good memory at school was the time I got to show the new teacher around the school. I felt pretty important. My not-so-good memory was being held back a year in fifth grade. I felt stupid, but I wouldn't tell the other kids that. After everybody else talked about some of their good and not-so-good memories, we got to start the counseling activity.

Dr. Nick brought out a poster with like a whole bunch of different faces of kids on it. I counted like sixteen different kids on the poster. I guess they were kids about my age. Each kid had a different face. One kid looked happy, another looked worried. One kid I noticed right away looked kind of sad and really pissed.

We were then given cards that had words like angry, excited, bored, lonely, afraid, happy, jealous, and frustrated written on them. Each card had only one word. Everybody got like four cards each. The counselor wanted us to take turns and match the word on the card with a face on the poster.

Dr. Nick thought it would be good if we looked at the cards he gave us and try to remember a time when we felt that way. He gave the example of having a card with the word lonely written on it. The counselor said to remember a time that we felt lonely either at home, in school, or with friends. Before we could match the card with the right face, we had to tell about the time we felt that way.

Roberto, one of the boys in our group, was dealt the shy card. Dr. Nick asked Roberto to think of a time when he felt shy. He also asked Roberto to try and imagine how he may have looked to others when he felt shy. After Roberto told what his thing about feeling shy was all about, Dr. Nick wanted Roberto to show the rest of the group his shy face.

Once Roberto had his shy face on, the counselor held up a mirror in front of him so he could see how he looks when he is feeling shy too! That was so funny and everyone began laughing, including Roberto! After everybody stopped laughing a little bit, Roberto was told he could tape the shy card to the picture of the boy or girl in the poster with the shy face.

This was turning into a fun thing because everybody got to do the same thing Roberto did like three or four times until no one had any cards left. I even told the other kids about how I felt so mad and sad when I was held back. Mostly, I just wanted to make the face in the mirror to get the other kids to laugh with me.

Dr. Nick wanted to know if being teased and feeling angry had anything to do with me hitting that one kid in our group when I was in the bus line. He showed me the embarrassed card and asked if that's what I was feeling now. I kept my head down and mumbled something like, "No...maybe."

Dr. Nick told us that sometimes it's very hard to tell the difference between certain feelings like anger and sadness. He said that sometimes a word like embarrassed can be used to describe both those words put together.

I was glad I didn't have to feel so stupid anymore about being held back. Dr. Nick said everybody feels embarrassed for lots of different reasons, and once you know everybody feels that way, you don't need to even feel embarrassed! He also said the look on our faces of how we're feeling might be confusing to other people too if we're not careful.

The counselor had two of the kids in our group do something he called a "face-off." Both kids sat in front of the group and were told to make their best happy, angry, and worried faces. We were supposed to vote on who could make the best faces that showed happy, angry, and worried but we couldn't. We were all too busy laughing!

Dr. Nick said he wanted us to practice talking about what we're feeling with our friends and family and then practice making faces in our mirrors that match how we're really feeling. He said the better we can do that, the better we'll be at figuring out how other people might be feeling too.

Dr. Nick also gave everyone homework to notice our family and friends faces this week. He said he wants us to talk with them about how they might be feeling, kind of like how he talks to us about our feelings. I remember he said, "That's what family, friends, and counselors are supposed to do and it's also one important way of showing people we care about them." When he said that, he pointed to the whiteboard and I knew exactly what he meant.

Dear Parent,

Your child attended a group counseling session today with several boys and girls. The purpose of the group was to help your child learn how to improve his or her abilities in identifying and expressing their feelings appropriately. For example, when feeling "angry," the counseling goal was not only to help your child identify the feeling of anger, but to also respond verbally and behaviorally to the feeling in a way that didn't make things worse for your child or anyone else.

SERVING THANKS

Goal of Activity: To help students understand and appreciate not only how fortunate they are, but to also realize how thankful they could be.

Student Mix: boys and girls of similar age and grade

Group Size: six to eight students

Suggested Time: thirty to forty-five minutes

Materials Required: serving tray, milk carton, table cloth, place mats, napkins, paper plates, plastic knifes, forks, spoons, construction paper, thank you cards, and pencils

Considerations:

This is obviously a good activity to present during the holidays. Many boys and girls are going to be able to relate this counseling experience to an actual experience they may have at home or in another family member's home. Sharing a meal during the holiday typically brings a lot of family members together; it may also bring about the awareness of family members who are no longer of this earth or those who are being treated in or detained in places such as health care facilities, prisons, or in the military far from home.

Holidays typically bring forth a tremendous amount of family issues. This is a good activity to help bring some of those issues such as abandonment, responsibility, and faith to the forefront of the student's awareness in a way that is optimistic, kind, and gentle. Sometimes, I think it's best to use this approach in addressing family dynamics and issues rather than always beginning the session with a direct investigation into family matters.

On one hand, this activity helps students recognize all they have to be thankful for, such as family, teachers, friends, health, food, clothing, shelter, etc. Underscoring this, however, is the counselor's attempt at promoting the student's awareness of appreciation for everything that is and isn't.

Student Reflection:

Dr. Nick came by my classroom this morning and asked if I wanted to be in group counseling. Duh? I was glad he came by to get me today instead of always just calling for me. I like that the other kids in class can see me go with the counselor. They think he's fun too. They got to know him a little bit a couple weeks ago when he came by my classroom and introduced himself to everybody. He stayed that day for a little while and told everyone what counselors do and how he helps boys and girls with different things by doing activities. He even did an activity with everybody in our classroom that day.

We stopped by some more classrooms trying to find the other kids in our group. When we finally got to Dr. Nick's office after some kids had to use the bathroom and get a drink, I saw a tablecloth and dinner place mats on our table. There was even a little carton of milk that he said not to open because it was rotten. Too gross!

Group got going with check-in. Family, school, and friends are the things we're supposed to talk about. Instead of talking about stuff that isn't so good, Dr. Nick said he wanted us to focus on one, two, or three positive things about family, school, and friends.

Dr. Nick let the youngest kid in our group go first in talking about her positive stuff. That girl was given a special paper plate. When she finished talking about family, school, and friends, she was supposed to give that plate to another kid who could get to go next. This kept going on until everyone checked-in. I'm pretty sure that this was the first time we've used something like a plate to take turns with and pass around during check-in. I liked it!

Our counseling activity started with Dr. Nick having paper plates and pencils for everybody. We passed the plates and pencils around the table until everyone got some. Dr. Nick asked that we use our plate as paper and use our pencil to write down the names of family, friends, and teachers who have been helpful to us over the past year. He said that helpful meant like helping us with stuff like school work or just hanging out with us.

It was good that the counselor said not to worry about spelling every name the right way. He said just to do our best so even if no one else could tell, we would at least know whose name we were writing about.

After like about a few minutes of writing people's names down, we had to stop. The counselor said he wanted us to share the names we had written on our plates with the other kids in group. Some kids read their names aloud while a couple kids just handed their plates to other kids to look at.

I was really pretty amazed to hear the names of so many parents, grandparents, relatives, teachers, neighbors, and of course, friends. One kid had twenty-two names!

Dr. Nick got us talking about the reasons it's important to tell people in our lives thank you for all they've said, done, or tried to do. He said that giving thanks is a really cool way of letting people know that we like what they have done for us.

The counselor then asked us to think about all the people in our lives who we can't say thanks to anymore. He told us to look at our plates and notice the names of people that weren't on it. What did he mean by that?

It helped that he asked us some questions about who those people might be because I couldn't think of anybody else. He asked stuff like:

How about the neighbor kid who moved to a new school?

Maybe it's the friend who left without a goodbye?

Maybe it's our teacher from last year who took a job some-where else?

Did anyone have a neighbor who helped you when you were home all alone?

Think about someone who left really suddenly and you were surprised and sad when you found out about it.

Him saying those things helped a whole bunch! Shayla, this one girl in our group, said that special person was her grandma who died. She started crying but she kept trying to tell the counselor how much she missed her grandma. Everyone told her that it was okay to cry and some of the kids gave her a pat on the back or a hug. George even gave her a piece of his own candy.

Dr. Nick said not much is worse than a leftover thank you, and a leftover-thanks usually turns rotten if it's not used pretty fast. He said it's sort of like having a glass of milk for someone, if you don't give it to them pretty soon, it gets gross and turns into stuff like guilt or regret.

The counselor gave a couple examples of how that type of guilt might feel. He said to try to imagine that guilt is kind of like an empty feeling that fills up with rotten milk inside of you and you can't get rid of it by throwing up either. He said the only way to get rid of the guilt feeling is to think of whatever the thing was that made you feel guilty to start with but only different. That didn't make any sense to me either.

Like the counselor told Shayla she should try to think of her grandma as having always known that her granddaughter loved her very much even if she never said but always wanted to. Lots of the kids in group agreed with what the counselor said, and one boy told the girl her grandma could be an angel in heaven who already knows everything. That made Shayla smile!

Dr. Nick brought a large serving plate to our table. On the platter was a really big-sized card with the word thanks written on it. Laying all around that card were lots of smaller thank-you cards. Dr. Nick told everyone to help ourselves to the cards and to take one for each name listed on our plate. I figured I'd take a whole bunch of thank you cards because they don't cost anything to give, and I bet the people I give them to might like them a whole bunch. ·

We sat around the table filling out our thank you cards. That was fun and I felt really good doing that too. Dr. Nick said to make sure we don't let these thank you cards turn into rotten milk, like the one he had sitting on the table. He also said to be sure and give them to the people that have their names on them as soon as possible.

I really had a lot of fun today. We all got to leave with our thank you cards. I even had one for my friend, Mr. Mike. He's the custodian at my school. He's kind of scary but I remember that he helped me get my bike unlocked one day. Some of the kids had so many cards that Dr. Nick had to give them a sack to put them in so they didn't get dropped or lost. It looked like everyone had lots of thank you cards to be giving out!

Dear Parent,

Your child attended a counseling group today with several other boys and girls. The group began with check-in. Check-in is a time we share information about our families, friends, and how school is going. The counseling activity we did today centered on becoming aware and showing appreciation for all the things and people we have or have had in our life. Ask your child to show you his or her "Thank You" cards.

BUGS

Goal of Activity: The student will be encouraged to identify events, situations, behaviors, etc. that bother him/her. Furthermore, the student will be taught relaxation techniques and will have the opportunity to practice the techniques as part of the counseling experience.

Student Mix: students of similar age and grade; gender mixing not advised

Group Size: four to six students

Suggested Time: thirty to forty minutes

Materials Required: assorted plastic or rubber insects

Considerations:

This is really a fun activity to direct. Students will enjoy taking their turn at placing bugs on their friends, as well as having bugs placed on them. Having a mat for the students to lie down upon will further assist in the relaxation process.

I suggest you separate the participants and conduct all boy and all girl groups. A portion of the kids you see in counseling may have unidentified inappropriate touching issues. We don't want to inadvertently create a bad experience for anyone in this activity. Take notice of how kids respond to the placement of bugs on their bodies. If appropriate, discuss how they may have felt as the bugs were being placed. I know this begins as a lesson in anger management but you can see how it might evolve into something more.

Be sure not to overwhelm the students with having to learn each step in muscle relaxation. Just getting students to learn how to walk away and lie down for a few minutes will be quite an achievement in itself! The school principal will be quite impressed if you can manage to get one or two of the more volatile students at school to independently go to the nurse's office and lie down the next time they feel like exploding!

Student Reflection:

Today was my day to go to school counseling group. Our counselor's name is Dr. Nick. He seemed glad to see me when I walked into his office. I could tell because he smiled at me and said he thought about me during the week. He told me he was proud of me and that it was important that I come to school, even on days when I'm not feeling 100% perfect.

After the other kids came to group, we talked about our goals for the year. One boy said he had gotten suspended during the week for fighting, but it wasn't his fault. He explained that he was being teased by another guy and his dad always told him he has the right to defend himself.

We all talked about that for a little bit because lots of parents say it's okay to hit someone if they hit you first. Dr. Nick said that sometimes self-defense can also be about walking or running away from possible violence now and then work at solving the problem later. He also told us that the person who hits back is usually the first one who gets caught. That's for sure! Everybody in our group talked all at the same time about getting in trouble for hitting someone who started the fight first.

During check-in each of us said something about our week at

school, with friends, and at home with our families. Dr. Nick wanted us to think of three things that bug or bother us too. One thing could be something that happens at home, another thing could be at school, and the third thing could be about friends.

Dr. Nick looked right at the boy who got busted earlier in the week for fighting and said, "Being teased might also be one of those things that bug us." Well, the kid didn't say nothing back and I saw the counselor just keep writing down a lot of our answers.

I was glad to be done with all that talk and start our activity. I got really excited when the counselor showed us a box of creepy, crawly plastic bugs and insects. He laid them out on the table for us to look at. He must have had fifty or more of those things! Even though all of us have stepped on, squished, and set fire to bugs before, we were told we couldn't hurt these little guys. Dr. Nick said we were going to treat these cool bugs as special pets called "peeves"! What the heck is a peeve? Dr. Nick said a peeve is just a name we give to special bugs.

Uh, yeah, whatever.

The counselor said we would be using the bugs to help us learn how to deal better with being bugged. Like he said, some boys and girls feel bugged when being called names. Other kids get bugged when they don't get picked to play in games. Two kids in our group said what really bugs them the most is when their parents argue and sometimes fist fight.

To start, Dr. Nick had us take turns practicing taking deep breaths and relaxing our face, neck, shoulders, arms, and hand muscles. He also taught us to repeat silently the words: "I can handle it, it's going to be okay."

The next part was really fun too! We took turns lying really still as possible on the carpet with our arms and hands against our sides. Kids in group got to take turns laying plastic bugs on the person lying down. While this was going on, that kid who was lying down was reminded over and over again of the three things that bug him.

We had some rules to follow about where we could place the bugs. They couldn't go under clothing or in any tickle spots like mouths, ears, belly buttons, and noses.

While we were taking our turns and lying there, Dr. Nick encouraged us to breathe deep and relax the muscles in our face, neck, shoulder, arms, and hands while repeating the positive words we learned earlier.

This was really a blast! I didn't mind that bugs were being placed on my face. Even though I tried not to laugh, I did sometimes and the bugs would fall off. Whenever that happened, that person's turn was over unless for sure it wasn't his fault. I was really careful the next time I had my turn and did my best at repeating the positive words.

Once everyone had their turn at being bugged, we had to go back to the table to talk about all the different bugs we used. Dr. Nick says that it is important to learn how to recognize and relax our bugging thoughts and turn them into positive thoughts before they turn into angry behaviors. The counselor also said that concentrating on keeping our bodies relaxed can help to keep our thoughts calm too!

The counselor looked again at the kid who had been suspended earlier in the week for fighting and said, "Jayden, it's okay to get angry, but it's important to learn how not to hurt yourself or other people when you're angry. That's what anger control and telling yourself positive things is all about."

I thought group was just about going to be over, but then Dr. Nick looked at me and was holding a bug in his hand. He told me that it bugs the school when I'm not in class because I'm supposed to come to school, even if I'm not feeling 100% great. I didn't think me missing school so much as something that really bugs people like my teacher, principal, and counselor before. Dr. Nick said that the school misses me when I'm not here, and it also really bugs my friends too.

When we left group, Dr. Nick let everyone keep a bug from the activity only if we'd promise to remember to keep our cool around all the things that bug us, especially things like our pet peeves.

At lunch today I got to play with Jeremy and Jacob. Those are two of the kids from my counseling group. They told me Dr. Nick talked to them after the rest of us left after group. They said something about him wanting to know more about them being bugged by their parents fist fighting. I told my friends just to relax about it...just like we learned in group today.

Dear Parent,

Your child participated in a counseling group today that dealt with "anger management." Plastic bugs were used to represent things that your child identified as being bothersome or "buggy." Relaxation techniques were also taught and rehearsed. Be sure to ask your child to show you the souvenir bug he or she received and to tell you about the new way he or she has learned to deal with stuff that "Bugs" him or her.

GIVING GIFTS

Goal of Activity: To help the student identify and be able to verbalize a heartfelt gift that he or she desires a family member or loved one to have.

Student Mix: boys and girls of similar age and grade

Group Size: four to six students

Suggested Time: thirty to forty minutes

Materials Required: gift identification cards, ribbons, and Christmas treats

Considerations:

Learning to become a responsible, kind, and generous member of our society requires kids to learn how to think about other people and family members' needs above and beyond their own. The holidays are a great time of the year for this to happen. Many of the boys and girls you may have in your counseling group, like many boys and girls anywhere, initially learn to think of the holidays in terms of receiving gifts. Generally speaking, that's not so unusual. At some point in time, however, it's beneficial for school-aged students to begin thinking about the needs, wants, and desires of someone other than themselves.

The activity is also designed to allow students to think about the needs of family members without the barrier of trying to finance their ideas. It also encourages the student to consider gift options that are less tangible. That is, things like time, hope, and a "magic 100% guaranteed cure" are certainly things that money can't buy. On this level, a student learns how to channel direct positive intentions into intellectual and emotional concentrated efforts. Prayer and positive wishes make for pretty great gifts.

Student Reflection:

Today was one of my better days in school. Not only is this our last week of school before holiday vacation begins, but I also had counseling group with our school counselor, Dr. Nick.

Our group had five kids in it, and I guess everyone was pretty much about my age. We did a pretty fast thing about our goals and then did check-in.

Dr. Nick wanted us to say something about how our holidays are connected to our families, school, and friendships. Like what do we do with our families to get ready for the holidays or if we ever have friends come over on a vacation. He even said we could talk about how our teacher gets ready for the holidays. I thought that was a fun way to do check-in. We got to talk about all that stuff and Christmas too!

Just when I thought we were going to do an activity, Dr. Nick gave us two questions to answer. The first question he said was like, "What's so good about Christmas?" The other question was, "Name one thing that makes celebrating Christmas hard?" Pretty much everybody knew the best part of Christmas was about getting presents. The hard parts of Christmas had lots of different answers.

Two kids said something about a parent being in jail or prison. Two other kids talked about going between their parents' new houses and being around people they don't know too good. It seemed everybody knew what it was like to get a present and have to pretend to like it!

I remember that Dr. Nick got some of those kids to talk more about how they felt not having their parents around and missing them. He also tried to get this one girl to talk about having to go to her step dad's house for Christmas Eve. I'm glad he knew how to make her stop crying after he made her cry in the first place.

On the whiteboard, Dr. Nick had drawn like this 3-D box. He drew one box for everybody in group. On top of the box he pasted a gift name card, like the kind you get on a Christmas present. He also stuck a real ribbon next to the card.

He asked us to put our heads down on our tabletop, put our hands together, close our eyes, and to think of someone in our family who really wants something a whole bunch. That something might be like a video game, shoes, or some kind of toy. He also said that it could also be something really important like a job, a refrigerator full of food, one more chance, or even something like more time.

I didn't know what he meant by a second chance or more time so I lifted my head up and said, "Huh?" He explained that the second chance might have something to do with a person wanting forgiveness for something he or she did. He said more time might be for someone like a Grandpa who is here just visiting from out of town or maybe for someone who is really sick and doesn't want to die now.

So once everybody figured out who was going to get what with their eyes closed and head down, Dr. Nick said to give him a thumbs up sign. I think he must have gone around and touched our thumbs. I know for sure he pulled on my thumb. If he touched your thumb that meant you went to the whiteboard to write the name of the person who was going to get a gift on the name card next to the ribbon.

The counselor then told us to draw a picture of what we wanted that person to have inside the 3-D gift box. I'm not much of a drawer, neither was anyone else. I could tell that Dr. Nick wasn't much of a drawer either. We got to help each other if anybody wanted help with their drawing.

Once all the gifts were drawn and we had put names on them, we took turns talking about who our presents were for. We also got to tell why we wanted that person to have the gift we gave them.

I'm not sure why, but I was glad to hear about all the presents the kids wanted to give people. It was really a fun feeling! One boy wanted his father to stay out of prison and had drawn his dad a picture of two fishing poles for his gift. He first tried to draw some dynamite but didn't want his dad to get into more trouble. The girl setting next to me told us about her present for her grandma. She had drawn a birthday cake in her gift box with one candle on it. She talked about how she wanted her grandma to have just one more birthday because she wasn't doing so good in the hospital.

I drew a Christmas tree in my box for my older brother. He's in a war someplace, and it's really hot in the desert he's in. They don't have Christmas trees there because they were all blown up because lots of people that live there don't believe in Christmas.

The counselor said even though he can't help us get the gifts we want to give, he can give us paper and color pencils so we can draw our gift for that person, just like we did on the whiteboard! Too cool! We even got to take the name tag and ribbon off the whiteboard and stick them to our papers!

All this stuff was really pretty cool. We got to take our papers with us, and Dr. Nick told us that no gift could be better than the ones we want...for someone else. He said sometimes it really works great when you just put your hands together, concentrate really hard, and watch to see what your heart tells your brain to do. He then gave us all a little Christmas sack with some treats in it and told us to have a great and happy Christmas.

Dear Parent,

The counseling activity for today focused on thinking about the needs of family members. "Needs" could be anything from "Just for fun" to "Can't live without." Boys and girls were encouraged not to be concerned with the financial constraints or reality of their choices. A gift could literally be anything! The activity today allowed your child to use his or her heart and mind in thinking about all of the people he/she loves that may be in need.

X'S AND O'S

Goal of Activity: This activity is intended to promote personal responsibility as the student learns to deal with the events in his or her life.

Student Mix: boys and girls of approximately the same age and grade

Group Size: four to six students

Suggested Time: thirty-five to forty-five minutes

Materials Required: colored erase markers, achievement pictures, disaster pictures, clipboard, and a dictionary

Considerations:

This can be a fairly time consuming activity. Getting answers from every group member for all three questions is going to take some time. Learning how to move quickly from one student to the next will be a helpful skill.

If you use the analogy of being held responsible for cleaning your room, even though you didn't create the mess, be prepared to hear the "That's not fair!" response. This is as good as any time to encourage students to begin examining their beliefs about fairness.

Remember, place extreme emphasis on the students' goals and the sustained effort it will take for them to reach those goals. Be supportive! These boys and girls may need to learn how to make good things happen. Perhaps, one of the reasons these kids are in counseling is because of an overabundance of less than fair events having transpired in their lives.

Some of your students may spend the next several years trying to clean up a mess in their life that had been created by someone other than themselves. This lesson is about supportive responsibility not passive victimization. Anything you can do at this early age to help your students deal responsibly and effectively with the stuff in their lives will be worth its weight in gold later on.

Student Reflection:

Dr. Nick had me be in counseling group this morning. By the time I got in his office, all the good chairs were being used by the other kids.

He told everyone thanks for coming to group and gave each of us a candy treat. The counselor said we could earn a second piece of candy by doing our best during group. He even promised he would give us one or two warnings or raise his eyebrows up and down if we needed to be reminded about having good behavior.

Usually our counseling group begins with check-in, but today we didn't. So instead of check-in, Dr. Nick just had a bunch of questions. First he asked us to talk about one of the best things we had ever done. He then asked us to name an important event that had a big impact on our family. He said a big impact might be something like having our house burn down, being in a car wreck, or winning a million bucks! His last question was about naming a friend who had moved away.

This one girl sitting on the other side of the table said the greatest thing she had ever done was to jump off a really tall diving board. Another kid said that his biggest thing had been winning a football throwing contest. Everybody had at least one big family story to tell. I heard about some people moving, some parents divorcing, and one kid whose dad died. What he said about his dad made me remember when my uncle got killed.

When it was my turn to talk, I told about my best friend who moved away last year. We'd been buddies since first grade. He moved because his mom was getting married again, and they were going to go live with his new dad's mom.

I think the counselor kept track of our answers on the clipboard he was holding. Once everyone had answered his questions, we got to start the counseling activity!

Dr. Nick drew a big circle on the whiteboard with a dot right in the middle of it. He said how the dot is kinda supposed to be me, and the circle around me is all about my whole life.

He said that each one of us lives in our own personal life. I think I understood what he meant, but I said, "What?" He said it again, and I think I understood better what he meant this time because he drew a circle for everybody and everybody was the dot inside their own circle.

Dr. Nick got out his clipboard and a red marker. He used the red marker and put a red X in my circle for all the things I told him during check-in that happened in my life. Like he put a red X for the time my friend moved away, the time my parents divorced, and another red X for when I got stuck in the elevator for three hours!

After he did that for everybody, he got out a blue marker. He used the blue marker and made a blue O for some of the things I told him about in my life that I did on purpose, like the time I called 911 to help my mom not get beat up by Ray. He put another blue O in my circle for the time I turned in a twenty dollar bill at school and another blue O for when I was our school's "Proud Eagle" of the month for reading a whole bunch.

The counselor put blue O's in everybody's circle for things they've done. He even gave that one girl in our group a blue O for the time she jumped off the high diving board. The whole whiteboard was full of circles, X's, and O's. Hey! Dr. Nick draws pictures just like my football coach does!

Our counselor said that each of our circles or lives is filled with lots of things. Some things we make happen, some things that just happen, and lots of other stuff too.

He then asked if any of us ever had to clean up a mess in our room even if we didn't make the mess. Heck yes! Just like all the time! That's when he had us look at the whiteboard again. He pointed to the X's in my circle and reminded me that even though I didn't have anything to do with my parents' divorce, I still have to deal with it because it's inside my circle. He said that for each of my red X's, and he did that same thing for everybody.

Nearly everybody said something about that not being fair, having to clean up other people's messes in our rooms. I thought it was kinda funny when Dr. Nick showed us his special dictionary. He looked up the word fair and showed us what it meant. It said something like "no such thing, a make believe word." Dr. Nick said that lots of times there is no such thing as fair, and we might want to think about that.

Dr. Nick showed us more pictures of things that just happen to people like tornadoes, hurricanes, floods, fire, and car accidents. He put a red X inside each of our circles on the whiteboard for those things too.

We all still wanted to talk about that not being fair, but the counselor said sometimes things just happen and we still have a responsibility to deal with those things too. I just about had a heart attack when he was looking at me and told me that sometimes people just die for no good reasons and it's not our fault but we still have to deal with being sad and stuff.

The only thing that started to make me feel better about growing up was when Dr. Nick showed us other pictures of good things. He said these good things are possible only if we make them happen. He showed us pictures of home runs, trophies, good grades, graduations, neat jobs, and sky divers. He marked a blue O for each of those things in everybody's circle on the whiteboard. My circle was now nearly completely covered with X's and O's.

Dr. Nick gave everyone a red marker and said we could go up to the whiteboard and add another red X if we wanted to. He said we could take turns and talk about one more thing that we have to deal with in our lives.

Only three kids went up. One boy said that he has to clean his room because his brother always gets it messy. Another kid added a red X and talked about always being late to school because his mom won't get up on time.

The one kid whose dad died wanted to talk about how it wasn't fair his dad died. The counselor said he's right. He also told the boy to try and stop being mad at things not being fair. Dr. Nick said that once you stop getting mad at things not being fair, you can start feeling better. I was surprised that he said that some kids might never get over someone dying and maybe the best they can do is just get used to it every day, but some days are just harder than others.

Dr. Nick gave everyone a blue marker and had us go up to the whiteboard and put an O inside our circles. He said that the O is going to be something good that we're going to make happen for ourselves.

One girl in our group said how she was going to go to college. Another kid said how he was going to become a professional wrestler. The boy next to me said how he would become a security guard and help his dad get out of jail.

Just as we were getting ready to leave counseling today, Dr. Nick put a blue O on the back of everybody's left hand. He said that was to remind us of things we can do for ourselves. He put a red X on the back of our right hand. He said that's a reminder of the things we have to deal with.

I thought I was done with counseling until next week so I was really surprised when Dr. Nick called me back to his office in the afternoon. He and I were the only ones there. He said he wanted to talk with me privately about Ray. He also gave me the red marker and asked if I had one more X to put in my circle. He said he could help me if I did.

Dear Parent,

Our counseling group began with check-in today! This is the time students' talk about their families, school, and friendships. After check-in, the boys and girls participated in a counseling activity. The activity encouraged students not only to take responsibility for the decisions they make and have made but also for the attitude and action they take in handling those decisions. Group members were further encouraged to apply some of those same concepts to the events other people have created in their lives too.

BRAVE, FOOLISH, COOL, OR GOOFY?

Goal of Activity: To help students understand behaviors in terms of categories and choices. Students will also be encouraged to recognize certain situations that influence decision making and practice making smart choices when it comes to choosing their behaviors.

Student Mix: boys and girls of approximate age and grade

Group Size: six to eight students

Suggested Time: thirty-five to forty-five minutes

Materials Required: TV/VCR/DVD, Warrior of Virtue film, index cards, juice packets, and popcorn

Considerations:

This is an easy way to help boys and girls evaluate behavior in a fun, safe, and non-threatening environment. Teaching a student how to evaluate behavior in terms of being brave, foolish, cool, smart, or goofy begins to provide him or her with the tools he/she will need to evaluate behavior.

Helping the student learn how to recognize his or her own behavior is important. Teaching students how to deal appropriately in situations where they are being provoked or pressured is critical.

Most boys and girls will experience provocation and the desire to show-off at some point in time during their school life. Certainly, some students will experience more pressure than others. When parent guidance and peer observation is not enough to help a child moderate his or her own behavior, school counseling may become the best option.

There are a host of movies available for the counselor to choose from that lend themselves toward conveying a sense of harassment. Use your own discretion. Be mindful that not all movies are recommended for the age of students you'll have in counseling group. A permission slip may need to be obtained before showing the movie you select. Regardless of the film selected, I find that having kids first listen to the dialogue heightens their curiosity for what is to follow. This is the moment you will find to be of greatest therapeutic value. How you proceed from here will determine how well the student understands the lesson.

Student Reflection:

Today I was in group counseling with Dr. Nick. Once a week he calls me to go to counseling. Even though most boys and girls like counseling, a girl from our group wanted to go to her music class instead of counseling. Dr. Nick went crazy when she told him that! Not really, I was just kidding. He reminded us that coming to counseling is a choice and sometimes choosing choices can be hard.

Well, that girl chose music class over counseling and the counselor told her it was a good choice for her to make. Dr. Nick said he would try and schedule her at a different time next week so she wouldn't have to miss music. The girl said she could miss math class next time for sure.

We sat around the table to start check-in and everybody was asked to say two things about family, school, or friendships. One of the two things had to be something good or positive and the other thing something that we want to get better.

One boy said his good thing about family was he was glad to

have seen his dad over the weekend. The wants better thing he said was that he wished his dad had spent more time with him rather than his step mom. Once everybody talked about their stuff, we got to start our counseling activity.

Dr. Nick gave everyone four blank cards. On each card a word had been written. The words were brave, foolish, cool, and goofy. On the back of each card was a definition about what the word meant.

We went over each card and what they meant. The counselor then wanted us to think of a time when we acted brave, foolish, cool, or goofy. We all had the chance to talk about some of the stuff we did.

E.J. told when he ran out into the street to get his football. First he thought he was being brave, but when the car almost crashed into him, I think he was feeling pretty mad and scared.

Our counselor then laid a towel over the TV in our room and told us to listen carefully. No one could see the movie he was going to play, we were only able to listen to it. What we heard only lasted a few minutes and it sounded like someone was being teased or dared to do something.

We got to listen to it again, but this time we were supposed to listen for examples of brave, cool, foolish, or goofy sounding behaviors. Dr. Nick said to hold up our brave card if we heard someone being brave, our cool card if we heard something that sounded cool, and to do that same thing for each card we had.

This was pretty fun. I had to listen really hard, but it was kind of exciting too! I think everybody had fun. Nobody really knew for sure when to hold up a card or not, but when one kid did the other kids did too.

It was good when Dr. Nick let us watch the movie we had been listening to. The name of the movie was called "Warriors of

Virtue." It was even better because he gave everybody a small bag of popcorn and a juice packet!

What we heard before really made sense now because we could watch it. This is pretty much what happened. This kid named Ryan, who was a little bit handicapped, was being picked on. These other kids were daring him to walk across a long, round tube. This tube thing was on top of a big tank of water that was spinning down into the sewer like a huge toilet swirly. It looked like if the kid fell he would drown. If he didn't walk across the tube, he would keep getting teased.

I couldn't believe that Dr. Nick stopped the film at the part where Ryan was on the beam and going across it when all this water came in from the top! Everybody wanted to know what happened next, but the counselor didn't let us see. He said we had to talk about it first.

Dr. Nick restarted part of the movie and asked us about the different actors and what they did. We needed to use our brave, cool, foolish, and goofy cards to talk about if they did any of those things.

Me and some other kids thought what Ryan did was pretty cool. The girls thought it was stupid. Dr. Nick said to use the foolish card for stupid things because foolish is pretty much a better word.

Dr. Nick gave everybody another card. This card had the word smart on it. On the back of it was a definition that read, "Being smart means making good choices that don't make things worse." Dr. Nick said that doing the smart thing won't always make us super popular, but it will make our teachers and families proud of us.

I sort of knew what that meant, but it helped that he gave some examples. Dr. Nick pulled out that sheet of paper he used to write down the stuff we said during check-in. He asked us about the answers we gave him about brave, cool, foolish, or goofy things we've done. He also wanted to know about what happened after we made those choices of being brave or whatever. He said what happens after we decide to do something are called "consequences."

Dr. Nick let us finish watching what happened next to Ryan. I couldn't believe he fell in! That was so stupid! No way would I have fallen! I do stuff like that all the time.

When counseling group was over, Dr. Nick asked everyone to talk about the activity with our parents. He also gave everyone a smart card to use whenever we wanted to. He gave me like ten smart cards and told me to be sure to use them as much as I can.

Dear Parent,

In counseling group today, your child was given a lot to think about in terms of choosing appropriate behavior. The issue of peer pressure was also examined through the role of a character approximately your child's age in a movie or script. We examined how peer pressure can effect a person's thinking and thus, their choice of behaviors. Be sure to ask your child about the differences between "Brave, Cool, Foolish, Goofy, and Smart" behaviors.

BULL'S-EYE

Goal of Activity: The student will be encouraged to consider the possibility that focusing on doing his or her best in any given activity may prove to be more rewarding than focusing only on a winning outcome.

Student Mix: boys and girls of similar age and grade

Group Size: four to six students

Suggested Time: twenty to thirty minutes

Materials Required: suction cup ball and marker

Considerations:

Some of the boys and girls you will have in counseling will experience difficulties in accepting outcomes. This is not only true for sports-related activities but also true for functions within the family and the classroom.

Helping students come to terms with understanding not only the limits and responsibilities of their preparation and effort, but how that effort may or may not influence certain outcomes will be an ongoing lesson for them throughout their lives.

As a counselor, you can use nearly any game for this activity requiring motor skill movement. Instead of the suction ball, dribbling a ball, jumping rope, and paddle ball have worked well in the past. However, there are two keys involved in choosing the right activity for this lesson. One key must be to choose an activity (or skill) everyone can do and, with practice, improve their ability level. The second key involves choosing an activity with an outcome that relies on more than just the skill and effort of the game's participants. That is, consider an activity that also involves uncontrolled variables such as wind, crowd involvement, the unpredictable bounce of a lopsided ball, officiating, or just plain luck.

Remember, the goal of this activity is to not only help students learn to handle undesirable outcomes but also to learn how to focus and maximize their time and energies on preparation.

Student Reflection:

I did counseling group with our school counselor today. We spent the first part doing check-in. I wish that one time we could just skip check-in and get right to the activity!

Dr. Nick told us we have to say more than "I'm fine" or "Everything is okay" when it's our turn to talk about family, school, and friends. He says the more he learns about our families, friends, and how we are in school, the more he can help us do better with those things.

Dr. Nick asked us if we had done our best during the past week. Like, did we really try hard at doing a good job with school work and our chores at home. Like most everybody else, I just try to get homework done. Sometimes I just want to get it done so I can go play. Sometimes I try to do both at the same time.

After check-in got done, we finally could start our activity.

The counselor told us we were going to be playing a game called Bull's-Eye. What we're supposed to do was to score the most points. All you had to do to win the game was to throw a suction ball at a target drawn on the whiteboard and get the most points. The closer to the center of the target you got, the more points you'd get. Like, the circle furthest away from the center was worth five points, the next circle closest to the bull's-eye was worth ten points. There was like four circles until you hit the center spot and that was the bull's-eye. The bull's-eye was worth twenty-five points!

Everybody got to throw the ball three times for their turn. Dr. Nick kept track of our points. After everybody was done throwing, the kid with the most points would be the champion. Dr. Nick said that everyone else would be given a pat on the back and told stuff like, "Nice try," "Good work," and "Better luck next time."

I was doing pretty good in the game, my throws always got points. If you threw the ball too hard, it wouldn't stick to the whiteboard and would just bounce off.

Tyler threw a fit! Two of his three throws didn't even hit the whiteboard and he ended up scoring three points total. Some kids called him a big baby and that only got him madder! Dr. Nick called timeout! Everyone had to go back to their chairs, sit down, and be quiet or we didn't get to finish the game.

Dr. Nick said that we needed to have fun but not to make fun of anybody. We had to put our heads down, close our eyes, and concentrate on having fun but not hurting anybody's feelings.

I could hear Dr. Nick whispering to the baby in our group who got so mad, but I couldn't hear what he said. I did hear the words, "relax, breathe, smile, and fun" though.

We got to play the game a second time, but this time the goal wasn't to score the most points, it was to do our best. Dr. Nick erased the numbers and all the circles except for the bull's-eye on the board so no one could keep score. Everyone got to throw the ball three times again.

With every throw, the counselor would tell us things like, "Great, good throw, great job, and perfect concentration." After everybody took their turns, Dr. Nick congratulated all of us a whole bunch for doing our best.

Dr. Nick told us to sit down at our table so we could talk about the game. We talked about how the two times we played the game were different. The first time we all played to win the game. The second time we played just to do our best.

I remember Dr. Nick said that sometimes playing to win and doing our best gets mixed together. Like, if we want to win a trophy or get an A+ on a test, we need to do our best. Here's the big but, he said, sometimes even if we do our best we won't always win the trophy or get the A+. When that happens, it's easy to feel like a loser even though we really did do our best.

Dr. Nick reminded us of that kid who got so mad when his throws didn't stick to the target. He gave the example of the kid wanting to win instead of doing his best. The boy's first two throws didn't stick to the whiteboard but his third one did. Dr. Nick said the kid focused more on what happened after he threw the ball instead of when he had the ball in his hand.

I remember the counselor saying, "Once the ball is out of your hands, anything can happen." He said some of those things that can happen could be stuff like the wind blowing, somebody knocking the ball down, or a referee making a bad call.

Dr. Nick told us that even if we don't always get first in something, we can always do our best, like what we did today that second time playing Bull's-Eye. He said it would help us to concentrate on how we do stuff instead of how things work out. Just like in juggling and throwing a ball and other stuff we've done, the counselor said our best will always get better the more we practice it.

Dear Parent,

In counseling today, we spent the first part of our group talking about family, school, and friendships. Students then participated in a counseling activity that promoted "learning to do their best" versus always having to win or be first. Many kids, despite doing their best, may never come in first place. Everyone, however, has control over how well they prepare to do their best. "Being first" compares your child to everyone else. "Doing your best" puts the focus right where it belongs.

THE CHALLENGE

Goal of Activity: To help the student understand the value in learning to make informed and level-headed decisions.

Student Mix: boys and girls of approximately the same age and grade

Group Size: six to eight students

Suggested Time: thirty-five to forty-five minutes

Materials Required: a four foot level, blindfold, and cushioned weights

Considerations:

A student will notice everything, including the look on the teacher's face. Remember, kids continue to notice your expression and tone long after you've stopped being aware of those things. From one counselor to another, be mindful of how you may come across to your students. It matters all the time and more than most educators realize.

The goal of this activity, like all activities, is another attempt at broadening student awareness. How you go about expanding the students' awareness is largely what determines how effective you, as a counselor, will be.

In the past, I have had great success with this activity helping students become more aware of their own, in the moment thoughts and feelings and how to make more informed decisions based on that awareness.

As the student takes his or her turn trying to locate the centering point on the level, begin placing very light weights one at a time on either end. In the absence of weights, try using two regular clothes hangers to attach to the level ends. On each hanger, attach a plastic bag, and inside the bags, you can place lumps of clay. Regardless of what you choose for weights, give each weight a name that describes the factor it represents. For example, one of the weights, depending upon the situation, might be called Dad's guilt or feeling lonely. Always wait for the student to make the attempt to adjust his or her centering point before adding another weight.

Helping the students become aware of the factors influencing their impending decisions and providing them with the skills and opportunity to process their thoughts is well worth the time this activity may require.

Student Reflection:

We were just getting ready to have a teacher ordered quiet time when the counselor called. I was on my way out of the classroom and saw my teacher was feeling better.

I got to group, and it was pretty much the same kids as last time. Sometimes a new kid joins if someone else is absent. Today, Dr. Nick had a new kid sit next to me. I told the new kid all about check-in and about the food the counselor passes out during group. The new kid said his name was Adam, and he had been in counseling at his old school too.

We did check-in. Some kids don't listen and distract me when it's my turn to talk. I told this one kid, "Shut up or I'll make you shut up." I had to move away from the group for two minutes.

I accidentally fell off my chair when the other kids were doing check-in. I had to stay away from the table for two more minutes. I guess it was okay that Dr. Nick showed me his watch to help me keep track of the time until I could come back to group. I got back just in time to get to answer a question the counselor gave everybody. He asked that we tell him one of the hardest decisions we've ever had to make about family, friends, or even something at school.

This one kinda sissy kid said that he sometimes has a hard time choosing which arm or leg he should poke with a needle to check his sugar diabetes so he can make sure he still has it. Savanna told about the time in court she had to choose between living with her mom or dad for nine months of the year.

When it was my turn, I felt a little stupid but I said my hardest choice was about what to eat first when we go out to a restaurant with lots of food sitting out for everybody to take. A couple kids laughed at me, and then I accidentally pushed one of those kids off his chair because I lost my balance. I had to sit away from the group for five more minutes, and Dr. Nick said, "Don't have any more accidents."

I saw Dr. Nick bring out a really long measuring level. He challenged each of the other kids in group to hold the level out in front of themselves with outstretched arms and try to get the air bubble lined up between the two other lines. This looked like it was going to be fun!

I accidentally started to get up from my chair, but Dr. Nick gave me his watch. I only had two minutes left!

It wasn't so hard, everybody did it pretty easy. Dr. Nick really looked surprised and kinda mad! He dared us to do it again, but this time we had to do it blindfolded! Just to make sure we would mess up, Dr. Nick said he was going to add weights to the ends of the level to even make it harder for us to balance!

Everybody got to try it like two or three times each. Some kids would get way off center, especially when the counselor added a weight to the end of the level. It was weird because if the weight was put on the left side, the kid would raise the left side way too much higher than the other side was. Nobody got it right in the center.

Dr. Nick made a line on the whiteboard. At one end of the line he wrote the words, "positive extreme," and at the other end of the line he wrote, "negative extreme." He said he knows some pretty extreme people, and they sometimes have a hard time finding a balanced point between the two extremes.

I didn't get what he was saying. I accidentally grabbed the level and told him I was going to try it one more time. I was really surprised that he said okay. He also said that accidents sometimes really do happen.

It was pretty cool having everybody watch me. I felt pretty cool! I had my blindfold on, and I could feel when Dr. Nick started to put these little weights on the ends.

The other kids started laughing when the counselor gave the weights he was putting on the level names. He called one roast beef. He called another pizza. He called this one really heavy weight pudding.

When Dr. Nick told me to find my centering point and be sure about what I want before I decide, I knew pretty much what he was talking about. He wanted me to be sure of what I really wanted.

The counselor said that finding our centering point is like making a good choice. Like, if somebody is standing there and someone is trying to start a fight with that somebody well that somebody might not notice that now he might do something extreme. Dr. Nick said that being scared might make that somebody feel like running and all the other kids standing around calling him chicken might make him stay and fight.

Dr. Nick reminded the rest of the kids about some of the hardest decisions they talked about earlier. Like with that one girl who had to choose between living with her mom or dad. Dr. Nick had her stand up, put the blindfold on, and try to get the level bubble in the center.

Just like with me, he gave each weight he put on the level a name. One was called guilt, another was called loyalty, and another was called time. Dr. Nick said that each weight can give us a lot to think about before we decide to do whatever.

Dr. Nick had that one kid with diabetes try the level again, but this time without the level! The counselor wanted him to imagine seeing himself holding the level and being right in the center before making up his mind about where to check his blood. That looked cool! It was fun when we all got to try and find our imaginary centering point.

Dr. Nick put the level on each of our heads and said he wants us to practice making level-headed, well-balanced, and even-tempered choices everywhere we go. He told me that being level-headed would also help me with not having so many accidents.

Dear Parent,

The counseling group began today with check-in. Check-in is the time your child has the opportunity to talk about how things are going with his or her family, school, and friendships. The boys and girls in group then participated in a counseling activity designed to increase their awareness of how emotions and other factors can effect their decision making abilities. We used a level to help illustrate the effects of making level headed, even tempered, and well balanced decisions!

BATTERIES INCLUDED

Goal of Activity: To help the student understand that the development of his or her inner qualities may lead to a greater sense of self-esteem and self-worth than solely relying upon physical appearance and topical talents.

Group Mix: boys and girls of approximately the same age and grade

Group Size: four to six students

Time Suggested: thirty-five to forty minutes

Materials Required: two remote control cars, identical batteries, pencil, paper, people pictures, and tootsie pops

Considerations:

This is a very interesting activity to conduct. Intuitive kids pick up on the message right away. For the students who are initially less intuitive, this activity helps to provide a bridge between not understanding and understanding the lesson. Once a student understands this activity as it pertains to self-worth, he or she will be inclined to suffer less through the insecurities of adolescence and beyond in the years to come.

Most children are more receptive than many adults are when it comes to exploring and believing in the unseen. The unseen, like the batteries in most electronic devices, can be said to represent our inner faith, beliefs, and values. Tapping into the student's beliefs and clarifying qualities above and beyond anything physical is at the core of this lesson.

In a world of physical differences, helping a boy or girl come to know and believe that he or she is, good enough and loved enough just for being who he or she is a great thing. Helping students learn to nurture their own innate abilities in becoming all he or she can become not only builds character and integrity now, but it also lays the foundation for confidence and improved self-esteem in the years ahead.

Student Reflection:

Group started with check-in today, kind of like it always does. I know what I'm supposed to talk about pretty much anything about family, school, and friends.

I couldn't wait to tell everybody about my house being broken into about three nights ago and the police coming over! Everybody was really listening hard to what I was talking about and wanted to know if I saw a gun or anything.

Our counselor wanted to know how I felt about our stuff being stolen and how maybe I didn't feel so safe anymore. He talked about how to call 911 and said feeling safe is just as important as being safe. He also wanted to know if anyone else ever had the police come over to any of their houses. Everybody in our group today either had the cops be at their house before or at a neighbor's apartment!

Because we all talked about crooks, cops, and staying safe, we didn't have time to finish check-in unless we wanted to skip our activity. Everybody voted for the activity!

Our counselor had one sheet of paper for everybody to use. We were asked to take turns and write down the names of things that used batteries. Dr. Nick said the hard part might be to not use what someone else has already said.

The boy sitting across from me went first and wrote down radio. He passed the paper to the person next to him. That girl got to write something, but it couldn't be a radio. She wrote cell phone. Everybody got to write at least three or four things before the counselor told us to stop.

Dr. Nick had this brown sack and brought out two remote control cars. One car looked brand new and really cool. It was fun, fast, and could do some really neat tricks! The other car looked pretty crappy and it didn't run very fast at all. It was slow and old and couldn't do anything but barely go forward.

It was fun when Dr. Nick picked some of us to drive the cars! Everybody wanted to be picked, but he only first picked the kids he said that were keeping their hands to themselves and not bothering others during group.

I don't know why, but the counselor then took the batteries out of both cars. He said he wanted us to notice what's on the inside of each car before he switched them. He took the old car's batteries and put them inside the new car and the new car's batteries into the old car.

Before he picked two new kids to drive the cars, he wanted to know if the cars would run the same or different. He made everybody guess an answer before the cars drove again.

Even though he switched the batteries, nothing changed with either of the cars. The newer car was still awesome and ran great while the crappy car still looked beat up and couldn't do anything very well. Everybody wanted to drive the new car!

Dr. Nick took the batteries out of both toys again and sat both cars on the table in front of us. He asked, "Is there really a big difference between the two cars now?"

We talked about that for a few minutes and everybody had answers. I thought they were both kinda broken without their batteries. They couldn't do anything really, so they were both pretty much worthless that way. This one girl thought she liked the new car better just because she liked how it looked.

We had to look at the batteries next. They looked the same. Dr. Nick said the batteries were probably made at the same time, had the same amount of energy, and came from the same company. He also said that if they're used equally, they'll last for the same time, that they all have the same markings and are probably the same temperature too.

Now he wanted to know if we thought the batteries were equal or different from each other. Well, after all of that, we said they were equal for sure!

When he asked us to choose either the batteries or a car as being more important, everybody talked at the same time! Jacob told the counselor his question wasn't fair. Dr. Nick showed Jacob the dictionary on his desk that said something about fair being a make-believe word.

This one smart kid that nobody likes too much said something about neither car is very good without the batteries. I said, "But the batteries don't do anything by themselves either." I thought that was a good answer, and I think Dr. Nick did too. He looked at me and said, "Good thinking."

Dr. Nick said that batteries are a lot like energy, and energy is just like strength. Without energy, neither car would be much different from each other. He said we might like one car over the other, but that's just what we like because of how we think it looks.

I didn't quite get this next part, our counselor said this activity could be about people too. I was thinking that people don't have batteries unless they're robots. Then that really got me thinking. What if Dr. Nick was a robot? What if my teacher is a robot? What if...? About then, Dr. Nick told me to listen.

He showed us magazine pictures of sports stars, rock stars,

presidents, parents, plumbers, and lots of people. He even had some school pictures of our principal and our teachers! Dr. Nick said that every picture he showed us is different from other pictures he showed us. Like how people look, dress, and sing and stuff. He said that just like with the cars, sometimes kids and grown-ups pick a favorite friend because of what they can do or how well they look.

Dr. Nick asked, "What does every person have inside of them that gives them their energy or strength?" Before anyone had a chance to talk about food and muscles and stuff, Dr. Nick gave everybody in our group a skinny battery to put in our pockets. For the kids without a pocket, the counselor told them to stuff it in their sock.

After everybody had a battery, he said to imagine that our pretend energy switch was turned off. Like we couldn't do any-thing except sit in our chair with our eyes closed and barely breathe. That meant we couldn't move or even think, we could only sit there.

After a couple minutes, he told us our energy switch was turned on. Now we could be ourselves! That meant we could think, move, talk, laugh, jump, smile, and breathe all we wanted to!

After we ran around for a little while, we traded our battery with someone else in the group. Once the battery was in our pocket or sock and turned on, we could go back to being ourselves and kept running around.

We sat back down at the table and the counselor brought out another sheet of paper. He wanted everyone to take turns writing on it just like last time. This time he wanted us to make a list of stuff that people find their energy or their strength in. He said that if we couldn't find anything, that might mean we have like dead batteries.

With the counselor's help, some of the things that we came up with were:

Believing in our families and friends

Being truthful and respectful

Being helpful

Knowing everything will work out for the best

Doing what's right

Knowing, even though people look different and can do different things, our important energy comes from the same place or common source like God

Remembering that we're loved and cared for no matter what we can or can't do

Dr. Nick said that it's important to keep our energy high because that's where our strength comes from. He looked at me and told me that if I kept my energy source inside me I would always feel safe and nobody, not even a robber, could ever take that away from me.

I understood that better when Dr. Nick said someone could always take your stuff, but just because they take your stuff doesn't mean they've taken something that's really important. The important stuff he said is the stuff you keep inside of you, like all the stuff you believe in.

When we left group today, everybody got their own flavored tootsie roll pop. Dr. Nick said just because they're all different on the outside doesn't mean they're not the same on the inside. He's right about my tootsie pop for sure! They all have the same center stuff inside of them. Once all the hard shell stuff is licked off, they all look the same! He said that just like the tootsie pop, we should always try to notice what's on the inside of a person first. That got me thinking about this kid in my class who sits in a wheelchair.

Dear Parent,

Your child attended a counseling session today with several other boys and girls. The activity was designed to help the student feel better about him or her self. The lesson de-emphasized the role of looking glamorous, wearing the "right" clothes, having to be popular, and being the best at everything. Your child was given a battery. See if he or she can tell you about the role the battery played in our activity, why everyone received one, and why his or her battery is just as good as anyone else's.

TOP SPIN

Goal of Activity: The student will be introduced to the concept of optimism. The student will also be encouraged to apply the concept of optimism to an event in his or her life and be provided the opportunity to rehearse the art of optimism for future reference.

Group Mix: boys and girls of similar age and grade

Size of Group: four to six students

Suggested Time: twenty-five to thirty-five minutes

Materials Required: soft plastic balls

Considerations:

The underlying issue in teaching optimism is helping students understand and believe in their own personal power to interpret events affecting their lives. In teaching optimism, you're not teaching a student to create a completely different reality, but you are helping that student learn how to think of difficult situations in the best possible ways.

Keeping in mind that even though optimistic people may become depressed and seek treatment just like everyone else, consider that a prescribed regiment of optimism in conjunction with the standard forms of treatment may also tend to decrease the severity and duration of depressive episodes in children as well as adults.

How you go about teaching optimism will largely be up to what you feel comfortable with. Whether you have the students spin a ball, find the silver lining to every dark cloud, or see the glass half full is just the first step in teaching optimism. Getting the student to practice optimism on a regular basis will be the biggest challenge.

One variation of this activity would be to turn the lesson into a friendly competition. For example, prepare a stack of note cards, with each card conveying a challenging situation. Read the card out loud and use a stop watch to keep track of how long it takes for each student to voice a positive aspect to the statement you've read. After three rounds, add each student's response time together. The student with the accumulated least amount of time can be placed in the top category of "Good-Better-Best."

Student Reflection:

There were six of us sitting in Dr. Nick's office for group this morning. Dr. Nick double-checked his list to make sure everyone turned in their counseling permission form. Some kid didn't have her form turned in, so Dr. Nick called the girl's dad. I guess it was okay after that because the counselor told Erianna that her parent said it was all right to go to counseling. Dr. Nick had her sign a piece of paper that read, "E.T. phoned home." I don't know why that was so funny, but Dr. Nick was smiling about something.

We started group with check-in. For check-in, we had to talk about family, school, and friendship stuff. Dr. Nick promised everybody a treat if they could answer his questions about each of those things.

Today Dr. Nick had lots of questions about our homework, attendance, chores, arguments with friends, brothers or sisters, and one thing about one hard thing that has happened to us. Like, the hard thing could be about having broken your arm, getting in trouble for throwing rocks, or having to move away.

I liked how we did check-in today because it was pretty easy just having to answer questions. Dr. Nick said he likes asking questions, but he also likes that we can think on our own and come up with our own stuff to talk about.

For activity, the counselor brought out a big box of colorful balls. You know the kind of balls you find in play land places. He gave everybody a ball, I got one that was green. I wanted a blue ball, but he said, "You get what you get." Before he even finished what he was saying, everybody else said, "And you don't throw a fit." I like telling people that better than I like hearing it. I said, "Fine...whatever."

All the counselor wanted us to do was to try and spin the ball on the table forwards, then backwards, and finally sideways. Too easy!

He said before any of us could spin their ball again, someone had to tell him what the word optimism meant. Even though he wrote it on the whiteboard, it didn't help. Nobody knew what it meant for sure so he told us what it meant. He said that optimism is a positive way to look at stuff that happens. Like if it was raining outside and you couldn't go out, using optimism, you would think, "That's okay, I can play video games instead." That was a pretty good example, but I liked it better when he said that optimism is like a hot, steamy iron because it smoothes the wrinkles out of your problems.

Now that we could play with the balls again, he told us to imagine that the ball we held in our hands was the hard thing we talked about during check-in. I wasn't quite sure what he meant by that, so I said, "Huh?" I don't think anybody else got it either because everybody else said, "Huh," too!

He tried to explain what he meant again, this time using an

example. He said, "To me, this ball in my hand is the time I lost my wallet. In my wallet were my money, driver's license, and credit cards." Oh! Why didn't he just say that in the first place? Everybody had to say what their ball was for them. Dr. Nick reminded some of the kids what they said earlier in group.

One kid said the ball was the time his dad was taken to jail, and another kid said the ball was the time his bike got stolen. The girl in our group asked if she could get a different ball because her parents are getting a divorce and didn't want to talk about it.

Dr. Nick said to put our ball on the table in front of us and that we were going to spin them. He showed us what he wanted us to do by doing that with his own ball.

We took turns spinning the ball he had given us. Sometimes the ball stayed on the table, and sometimes it didn't. I guess it didn't matter so much. Dr. Nick said the only thing that matters is learning how to put a spin on the ball.

After everyone practiced spinning their ball, Dr. Nick told us how he was able to use optimism and put a positive spin on the time he lost his wallet. He said he canceled his credit cards, which was no big deal, and got a better picture on his driver's license. He said he only lost a couple bucks that he would have spent on nothing important. Then he talked about how he could get a really neat looking new wallet now that his old one was gone.

The counselor said that we could use optimism like an iron to flatten out some of the rough spots on whatever to make them kinda smooth with something positive. Like with the kid whose dad went to jail, the kid figured out his dad might get some counseling to help him with his anger problem. Being in jail can also get his dad to stay off drugs, and his dad could also get some more real cool tattoos. Erianna, the girl in our group whose parents split, talked about how she got to move here with her dad and came to this school and met her new best friend.

Dr. Nick helped some of the kids find something good about the bad thing that happened to them. This one kid said that nothing good happened when his dog ran away from home yesterday. Dr. Nick told him that sometimes it takes a little bit of time to smooth out some of those things.

Everyone got teamed up with another kid. We got to take turns throwing and spinning our balls back and forth to each other. We did that lots of times and got pretty good at it.

It was funny because we had to say what the ball was about to start with, and then we had to throw and spin the ball to our partner. When our partner caught the ball, we had to tell them what our positive spin was about.

Dr. Nick told me that the spin I put on the ball didn't really change the ball, but it did change how I feel about stuff the ball was about. He said I can't always control what happens, but I can learn how to control how I think and feel about those things and that just makes the ball easier to hold on to. He said it's just like ironing the wrinkles out of your shirt, it doesn't change the fabric but it does make it better to look at.

Even though I didn't say nothing about it in group, maybe I can think about my sister moving away from home and being in the Army to like now maybe I can have her room!

We got to keep the balls we used in counseling today! Dr. Nick said he wants us to keep practicing putting a spin on our problems. He also told us to play catch with our friends and parents so we can teach them how to spin stuff too.

Dear Parent,

Your child participated in a counseling group today with the school counselor. The focus of the counseling group was to help your child learn about "optimism." The counselor used a ball to help your child understand the art of putting a "positive spin" on difficult or negative events. Students had the opportunity to identify a difficult event in their lives and practice putting their best spin on it. The counselor gave everyone a ball to keep and practice with as a reminder of the lesson.

WORKING TOGETHER

Goal of Activity: The student will have the opportunity to be successful in learning how to work with another person toward a common goal.

Student Mix: similar age students with discretion for gender mix and pre-existing conflicts

Group Size: six to eight students

Suggested Time: thirty to forty minutes

Materials Required: over-sized button down shirt, over-sized zippered jacket, a boot with laces, and treats

Considerations:

This activity helps to develop interpersonal skills, improve patience, and increase an individual's sense of belonging. It promotes not only respect for the self, but also a sense of appreciation for the people the student works with.

This is a good activity to help boys and girls understand how important working together is. Be mindful when pairing students together of any pre-existing antagonistic relationships. In some cases, when a student has to work with someone they're not getting along with, the shared experience of working toward completing a common goal may be enough to overcome their differences. I would, however, be careful of putting two kids together in the same coat that earlier in the day got into a fight and sent to the office. Regardless of what you decide to do, it's nice to know where the nurse's office is.

Instead of using a jacket, sweater, and shoe, consider going outside on a nice day and have the kids participate in a potato sack event, a jump rope activity, basketball drill of rebound and shoot, or some other cooperative endeavor. No matter what events you choose, be creative and have fun when you start planning your own activities. The more fun the kids have, the more likely they are to remember the activity and on some level, what the lesson was all about.

Student Reflection:

Once a week the counselor wants me to be in counseling group with other kids. I usually have a lot of fun when I go to group, but sometimes I feel like I'd rather stay in my classroom with everybody else, especially if we're doing a game or something different. We weren't doing nothing different today, so I was glad to get out of there.

Sometimes, I just meet with my counselor by myself before the other kids show up to talk about stuff that I'm not so good at. Today he asked me how I'd been getting along with the other kids at school. I wasn't going to tell him I had been suspended unless he asked. He asked about my attendance, being on time, homework, and grades. Whew! I was off the hook!

Dr. Nick called for the rest of the group once we were finished talking. As the boys and girls came in, I pretty much knew who everybody was except for one girl. Dr. Nick had everybody stand up and say our names, grade, and yuckiest icky thing. My thing was walking barefoot and stepping on a slug!

Group started with check-in. Every week the same kids in our group try to get by with barely saying much about their families, or school, or other stuff. Dr. Nick always makes them talk. He tells them to either have fun and participate or go back to class. It's kind of a fun joke the way he says it, the other kids smile and then tell him all sorts of stuff.

I'm glad he tells me to talk about my family, even though I usually like to keep things to myself. One day, maybe some day pretty soon, I'll tell him about how embarrassed I feel when my parents yell loud enough for the entire world to hear.

After check-in was done, we got to do our activity. Dr. Nick had us choose a partner. Once we had a partner, we had to do things as a team. The first thing was to zip a jacket, the second was to button a shirt, and the third thing was to tie a shoe.

What made doing this stuff so hard was that each team had to work together. Like, one member of the team could only use his right hand, while the other member could only use his left hand. This was weird because it was both frustrating and funny at the same time! Everything we did seemed to take forever to get done. Dr. Nick just kept telling us we were doing good and to do our best.

My first partner was this kid I know from the classroom across from mine. We both put on the jacket to begin the activity. His left arm was in the left sleeve, my right arm was in the right sleeve. We stood really close together so the jacket could go around us. Zipping it was tough but we got it. I thought we did pretty good, but for sure, some kids didn't do so good as us. I was way glad I didn't have to have this one kid I don't like so much as my partner.

After we all did that first thing, we had to change partners. Nuts! Dr. Nick put me with the kid I didn't like! I felt like not doing it, but I did it anyway so I could get candy later.

Well, I was the left arm and he was the right arm once the shirt was on. Trying to get it buttoned was making me mad! He wouldn't do what I was thinking he should be doing! Dr. Nick told us maybe we could take turns being the buttoner. We didn't do so bad I guess. Our time was better than most. That kid put up his hand for me to give him a high five. I gave him a high five, but I'm pretty sure I didn't smile though.

Our final thing was trying to tie a shoe. We changed partners again, and the counselor gave each team a super large boot to lace and tie! This boot had like thirty lace holes to fill up. The rules stayed the same, my partner could only use his left hand and me my right hand. This was really frustrating, but I was kind of liking it too! It's hard to do something like this with everybody watching. I started to feel angry when I felt my partner wasn't trying very hard. I looked at Dr. Nick who was looking straight back at me and telling me I was doing a great job and to be patient.

Once we finally got done, Dr. Nick had us sit at the table to talk about all the stuff we just did. After a little bit, the counselor helped us figure out that working together means you have to talk and listen, be patient, and know you've both got the same goal.

Dr. Nick said that learning to work together is very important, especially in school. We didn't have to raise our hands or nothing, but he said we should answer some questions in our own heads. Dr. Nick asked, "Who in this room sometimes has a hard time getting along with other kids?" He then asked, "Has anyone in this room ever been suspended from school for not getting along with other kids?" Some kids started pointing at one another, then someone pointed at me! The counselor told us to put our hands down. He said that the only people who need to know probably already know.

Dr. Nick told us that not all the stuff we have to do with a partner is going to be easy. He said that some stuff, especially things in school and at home, takes a lot of effort with someone to get done. He told us that the hardest thing we might have to do is just hang in there with the person we're working with and that the goal would take care of itself.

We had to come up with a list of things that take more than one person to do. We could only choose from stuff at school and at home. Dr. Nick used the whiteboard to keep track of our answers. Doing dishes, laundry, and yard work were the most usual answers. Dr. Nick asked, "Who works best in your house together?" In my house, it's best if my dad doesn't drink beer and whiskey when he's working with my mom. They just don't work very good together, I thought to myself. I was too embarrassed to say anything out loud.

When we were getting ready to leave counseling, Dr. Nick had us do one last challenge. He gave a Payday candy bar to each team to share. Our challenge was to work together, just like last time, to take off the wrapper and break the candy bar in half without dropping it on the floor.

I couldn't believe that one kid picked up and started eating the piece of candy that fell down on the floor! I would have been too embarrassed to have done that! He just blew if off and popped it in his mouth like it was no big deal! Dr. Nick told me that maybe things aren't always as embarrassing as I always think they are.

Dear Parent,

Your child attended and participated in a group counseling activity today. The activity focused on the importance of "teamwork." Teams, consisting of two students each, were given a variety of tasks to complete within a limited amount of time. Three things your child came to understand about this lesson were: 1. You have to try hard, 2. You must communicate, and 3. Be patient! Just ask your child about how complicated tying a shoe with a partner can be!

MYOB

Goal of Activity: To help the student understand the differences between reporting, informing, and minding his or her own business.

Student Mix: boys and girls of similar age and grade

Group Size: four to six students

Suggested Time: thirty to forty minutes

Materials Required: list of questions, statements, and citizenship awards

Considerations:

As a counselor, I have found this activity to be relevant to boys and girls of all ages. I think it is important to teach boys and girls at an early age about learning to differentiate between situations that require reporting, informing, or minding their own business.

During check-in, you will find it common that students report on things outside of their immediate support systems of family, school, and friends. Be careful as you guide the students back to focusing on just their support systems. Students often prefer to set their attention on things that intentionally take the focus off of them and subsequently from the things they need to be working on in group.

Confronting students too harshly or abruptly in your attempts at helping them refocus on their primary support systems and issues may cause the student to either shut down or develop another evasive maneuver called the "Everything is fine" response. Remember, this is a fun activity and kids will learn from you when and where to say, "MYOB!"

One variation of this activity would be to have students develop a list of their own situations involving reporting, informing, or minding their own business. Using a tape recorder to play back the students' comments and responses not only adds quite a bit of excitement to the activity, but also provides a greater sense of credibility to the acts of reporting, informing, and learning when to…"Mind Your Own Business."

Student Reflection:

I went to see Dr. Nick for counseling today. During group when we were doing check-in, the counselor stopped everything really fast! He said that some of us weren't really talking about our own families, friendships, and school stuff.

The counselor looked at this one goofy girl and said, "What you told us about the neighbor getting into trouble with the police is interesting, but what does that have to do with you?" To Ryan he said, "What you said about that girl farting in the library is okay, but what does that have to do with being important to you?" The counselor said things like that to nearly everyone. He wasn't being mean, he just sounded like he didn't get it.

Our counselor asked us if we knew what the letters MYOB stood for. Pretty much everybody knew they stood for "Mind Your Own Business."

Dr. Nick wrote the letters MYOB on the whiteboard and then wrote two other words: report and inform. Dr. Nick said that the big difference between them is that if we're going to report something, it's got to be important and urgent, like right now! Informing, he said, is also important but it doesn't have to be right now. Dr. Nick said another way to help tell the difference between reporting and informing is that sometimes informing might sort of sound like people spreading rumors or gossiping.

We got back to doing check-in, and it seemed like everybody did a good job just talking about their own stuff.

We did a game for our activity today. Dr. Nick said the game was going to be about listening, thinking, and picking the best answers.

Dr. Nick opened his notebook and read a question or said a statement from a list he had made up. If what he said sounded like something that needed to be reported right now, we would hold up one finger. If it sounded like something that someone should just know about, we would hold up two fingers. If his question or statement sounded like we should MYOB, we were told to close our eyes, put a finger in each of our ears, and keep our mouths closed. Too funny!

He had us practice putting one finger up in the air to report, another finger on the opposite hand up in the air to inform, and if the statement sounded like we needed to mind our own business, we put a finger in each of our ears. Dr. Nick said be sure not to use our middle fingers to hold up in the air because that wouldn't be good, and it might send the wrong message to people around us. He also said that we should only shove our fingers in our own ears.

This sounded like we were going to have a lot of fun, and I had a hard time sitting still until he began reading the questions and stuff. Dr. Nick wanted everybody to sit as still as we could and to really listen to what he was going to be reading. He didn't start reading until everybody was listening.

Some of his questions were easy to figure out, but some were pretty hard. Like, he said some of these things:

If your home is on fire, would you report it immediately, casually tell someone, or MYOB?

Your friend just cheated on a spelling test. Would you report it immediately, casually inform your teacher, or MYOB?

You just heard that a student was going to pull the fire alarm during lunch. Would you report it immediately, casually/sorta inform/tell someone, or MYOB?

You heard there would be a fight after school today. Would you report it immediately, casually inform your teacher, or MYOB?

You think your father has been drinking alcohol even though your mother said he better not be. Would you report it immediately, casually inform your mother, or MYOB?

You overheard two students talking at lunch. One of the students said she was planning on running away from home after school today. Would you report it immediately, casually/sorta inform/ tell your teacher, or MYOB?

As you were walking down the sidewalk, you found a plastic bag filled with something you thought were drugs. Do you report it immediately, casually inform a parent or teacher, or do you MYOB?

A note was given to you from a classmate to pass along to someone else. Do you report the note immediately, casually tell your teacher, or do you simply MYOB?

You heard someone likes your best friend. Do you report it immediately (to your best friend), casually tell someone else, or do you MYOB?

You discover an inappropriate/naughty magazine in your

sister's room. Do you report it immediately, casually/sorta inform your dad, or MYOB?

It was fun for each thing he read! Dr. Nick kept track of how many times I put both fingers in my ears. He told me I really need to work more on minding my own business and that keeping my sister's magazine was not one of the choices.

We talked about those questions he read. I'm not sure why but everybody remembered like a thousand other things that had to do with reporting or just telling somebody something.

Pretty much everyone knew when to report stuff because they were emergencies. Just letting somebody know what was going on, like when to inform somebody of something, was a little harder to figure out. Dr. Nick said we could use the trouble rule to help us know if we should inform or MYOB.

The trouble rule is thinking, Why am I doing this? If we tell somebody what's going on is it because we want to get somebody in trouble? If the answer is yes then we should probably MYOB. If the answer is no, then maybe we should tell someone.

Because we still had some time before we had to go back to class, Dr. Nick wanted us to talk about if we ever had to report an emergency. One kid said he called 911 when he heard his neighbor yelling at his dog and hitting the dog with a stick. I guess that was the right thing to do, because the counselor said he understood why the boy called.

When we were leaving group, Dr. Nick gave each of us a special paper. He said it was a "Citizenship Award," and he read it out loud and told us to take it home and put it on the refrigerator. The award had this written on it:

M any times in your life you will need to know when not to get involved.

Y our decision will be based on what you've learned, think, feel, and want.

O ften your mood may influence what course of action you take.

B e careful, for whatever your decision may be it will have an effect on you, your reputation, and your relationships with family and friends.

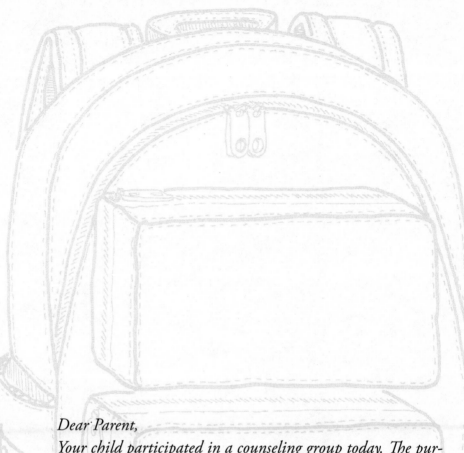

Dear Parent,

Your child participated in a counseling group today. The purpose of the group was to help the boys and girls learn how to improve their skills at "Minding their own business!" Many boys and girls can get themselves into serious trouble when they think they're doing the right thing. Today's activity was designed to help your child learn the differences between, reporting emergencies, casually informing adults of important situations, or just simply when to "M.Y.O.B."

THE BIG EXPERIMENT

Goal of Activity: To help broaden students understanding of the effect colors and music can have on their emotions, thoughts, and memories.

Student Mix: boys and girls of approximately the same age and grade

Group Size: six to eight students

Suggested Time: forty to fifty minutes

Materials Required: compact disc player, music CD (Adagio for Strings-Barber), overhead projector, color slides, stop watch, pencil, and paper

Considerations:

I like this activity because it indirectly and gently allows participants to search their minds for past and present emotional hot spots in their lives. Hot spots have the potential to be favorable or unfavorable, depending upon the student's interpretations of those particular events. That's why it's important to encourage the student to elaborate and/or investigate their memories.

In helping this activity unfold, remember most students in school have been exposed to the rigors of standardized testing. Remind your students that in some ways this experiment will be no different. Allow the members in your group about one minute to write down the names of people on their lists. Be sure to emphasize that correct spelling isn't important in the outcome of the experiment. You may also want to clarify what "names of people you *know* that come to mind" means. An alternative statement might be all the people you know that you can think of. Let the kids know that the uses of proper names are not necessarily needed. For example, using the name Dad is just as good as using dad's actual first name.

Using instrumental music to help facilitate emotional memories is a good tool for the counselor to learn. In this activity I use "Adagio for Strings" (Barber) performed by the Los Angeles Philharmonic Orchestra, conducted by Leonard Bernstein. I chose the selection because the music encourages the mind to wander, and this is precisely what the student's mind needs to do. It then becomes our job to help the students explore their emotional memories and, when necessary, help the students adjust or re-adjust to the impact and role those memories may currently be having in their lives.

Student Reflection:

I was just sitting at my desk and looking out the window when our classroom phone rang. I'm not sure what the other person said, but my teacher said, "Anytime is a good time." It was Dr. Nick!

On my way to the counselor's office, I saw other boys and girls from our group going to the same place I was going. We started running to see who would get there first. Next thing I know, Dr. Nick is having us go back to the place we began running and have us walk to his office. I didn't realize he was standing outside his door watching us.

When we got in his office, he said something about walking being safer than running. I was trying to hurry to find the best chair to sit in and didn't hear him finish whatever it was he was saying.

Once we all sat down, Dr. Nick gave everybody a handshake. Some of the boys and girls gave him a hug. He told us thanks for coming and then passed around a bowl of treats. Dr. Nick usually wants us to have a treat for coming to group and told us we could earn another treat by doing good in group.

We started check-in with the person at the counselor's right-hand side and went all around the table. It was pretty neat doing it that way. We had to keep a certain order. Like, the first person said something about family. The next person had to say something about school, and the next person talked about their friendships. We went around the table like three times, and everybody got to talk about all that check-in stuff.

Dr. Nick told us that we were going to be in an experiment today and that the experiment would be our activity. The counselor said that he couldn't say too much about the experiment until after the experiment was over. He did say that doing this experiment would be like taking a test. Dr. Nick told us that everything would be fine as long as we were willing to follow simple directions. I thought we were going to be using the Bop it toy again like that one time. I shouted out to everybody that's what we were going to do, but I think I heard Dr. Nick sorta growl and for sure he said no. Everyone said they would do the experiment. It started with everyone having a pencil and sheet of paper labeled A on top of the table. A second piece of paper labeled B was put under our chairs.

The counselor had turned off the phone, placed a do not disturb sign on the door, and turned down the office lights. He made sure each of us had two or three tissues in case we needed them. I'm glad he gave me a couple of tissues because of the cold I have. I'm glad he did that too because even though I was wearing a long sleeve shirt, sometimes it's just not enough.

Dr. Nick began reading directions. Pretty much, he said: "In the next few seconds you will be asked to write down the names of people you know that come to mind. You will have a certain amount of time to do so. Write until you are instructed to put down your pencils."

The counselor then told us when to start writing. After I guess like a minute or so, we were told to put down our pencils and to place our paper inside our pockets and leave them there until later when we'll be told to bring them out.

We were told to sit quietly and watch the overhead screen. Dr. Nick showed us color slides. Each slide was a different color. Each one was shown for like twenty seconds. After like maybe the sixth slide, Dr. Nick showed another slide with the word red written in black. What's up with that? I started to say something out loud, but he looked at me and shook his head.

The counselor then gave the direction to rest our heads on our tabletop and to keep our eyes closed until we were given further instructions. As soon as our heads were down and eyes closed, we heard music being played and my nose started to run. At the beginning of the music, the counselor said: "Clear your mind of all thoughts, and allow the music to discover where your thoughts need to be."

I had no idea what that meant so I raised my hand. He didn't call on me but he did say: "Don't try to think of anything, just relax and listen to the music." That made way better sense.

I didn't recognize the music being played. It was way too relaxing for me, even boring. At times I felt like falling asleep, and maybe I even did. You know what? I was way glad he gave me those Kleenexes earlier because my nose was running a lot more than my sleeves could take.

At the end of the music, which seemed like a million years later, Dr. Nick said to stay quiet, open our eyes, and sit up. He then said to quietly reach down and grab our paper labeled B from under our chair and put it on our table to be ready to write on.

He said, "In the next few seconds, you will be asked to write down the names of people you know that come to mind. You will have a certain amount of time to do so. Write until you are instructed to put down your pencils." That sounded just like the same thing he told us to do the first time. I started to say something again, but then he just repeated what he said. So, I just wrote down the names of people I had been thinking about. At the end of about one minute, we were told to stop writing. Dr. Nick then congratulated us on doing the experiment!

The lights came back on, and I got to take the sign off the door and turn the phone ringer back on. Dr. Nick told us he could now talk about what we just did. He also wanted to know what we thought about the experiment too. The counselor said this experiment was partly about helping us understand what music and colors does to our brains.

I knew this activity wasn't as fun as most the other counseling stuff we do, but I also know he was trying his best to help us figure this thing out about colors and music.

Dr. Nick said that for most people there would be some repeats between the two lists of names we made, but there would also be some big differences too. Like, List A names might have the names of people that are on our minds right now or not too long ago. List B might have the names of people that make us remember lots of strong memories.

Dr. Nick also said that List B names have to be on List B because if they were on List A we'd either be happy, mad, or sad all the time and all at once.

I still really didn't know for sure what he was talking about, and I'm sure I looked like I was bored, so it was good that he told all of us to hang in there just a little bit longer.

I got into the activity a lot more once he started to ask questions about our lists! Some of his questions were:

Which of your lists has the most number of names?

Does anyone have the name of someone on List B that you have not seen or thought of for a very long time (past best friend or relative)?

Did anyone list the name of a dead person on List B or a person who died recently on List A?

Did anyone write down the name of a pet on either list?

While doing List B, did anyone have the experience of thinking of someone but refused to write down that person's name (negative memories and unwanted emotions)?

In looking at your lists, is anyone surprised about forgetting someone's name from either list?

Did anyone write his or her own name?

Does anyone have the name of a person on List B who says he or she is one thing, for a example friend, but you know different?

Did anyone remember ever having been tricked or lied to?

Did the quality of writing change much between anyone's two lists?

How many matching names did the two lists have?

Dr. Nick was curious about our thoughts during the music and how we felt while the music was being played. He said sometimes people who do this experiment have told him that their mind and feelings go to people and places they love to remember, or sometimes really try to forget about.

That's for sure! One kid remembered going to his grandmother's funeral a long time ago. His grandma didn't make List A but she did make List B! Another kid, this one girl, started crying a little bit and even looked mad. She told Dr. Nick that she remembered when her parents were divorcing a couple years ago. She said she remembered what that was like but didn't like remembering it. She had written the name of the town she lived in then on List B.

During the music I thought of my best friend from first grade. He made List B but not List A. Dr. Nick thought the reason my friend made List B was not only because I like him, but I've learned how to live every day pretty good without him, and I don't always have to think of him.

Dr. Nick asked us what we thought about the slide that had the word red written in the color black. That's right! What was up with that? He then said to check List B for a name of anyone who says they're one thing but they're really not. Like a friend or relative who says they have your best interest in mind but they sure don't act like it! The counselor said that's a mixed message for sure.

Here was the pretty cool part. Dr. Nick said that once I let my thoughts go free to wherever my mind wants, my thoughts will usually go to people or places that I have strong emotions toward and that could be something good or bad. Dr. Nick said that's what the music and colors help do. They help our thoughts go where they need to go so we can remember things that are really important to us or remember stuff that we still need to deal with better and learn from.

Everybody talked like crazy about the stuff on their lists and a whole bunch of memories we've had. Dr. Nick said maybe like one reason everybody seems to start remembering stuff on long car drives is because of all the colors we see and music we hear along the way. That always happens to me! I couldn't even believe he told us to go back to class and that group was all done!

Dr. Nick gave everybody a second treat for doing our best in the experiment. He said to be sure to tell our parents about what we did and to show them our lists, even if their names weren't on them.

Dear Parent,

Just a quick note to inform you of the counseling activity your child participated in today. The activity was intended to help your child understand how music and colors can effect thoughts and mood. In our "experiment," your child developed two lists of names. One list was developed before hearing music and seeing colors, the other list, afterwards. It was interesting how different the lists turned out to be! Be sure to ask your child about his or her thoughts and memories while the music was being played!

THE GAME

Goal of Activity: The student will participate in a process that encourages good decision making in a game, limited only by their answers and the uncertainty of time.

Student Mix: boys and girls of approximately the same age and grade

Group Size: four to six students

Suggested Time: twenty to thirty minutes

Materials Required: checkerboard, tokens, treats, and die (one dice)

Considerations:

This is a good activity because it's easy to pull together on short notice. You can always tailor your questions to the age of your group members as the lesson moves along, but you can start the activity with the questions provided in the student's narrative.

Certainly the goal of this lesson is for students to learn the importance of good decision making, but in a subsequent goal, this lesson also provides the student with a link to a world that doesn't always have answers.

There is a significant amount of ambiguity embedded in this lesson involving time, direction, and specific outcome.

Helping a student learn how to accept some of life's uncertainties and be responsible for the choices he or she makes along the way will, in the long run, be of great benefit to the student. However, motivating and encouraging a student to do his or her best regardless of not knowing or understanding the rhyme or reason as to the events unfolding in his or her life is probably the greatest lesson of all.

Student Reflection:

I met with Dr. Nick today for group counseling. We had some new kids in group. The counselor said that it's good to meet and get to know some new kids who might turn out to be our best friends one day.

We started group like we usually do with check-in. Dr. Nick had us talk about our family, school, and friendships. He also had us go over our goal cards.

A couple kids had the goal of making new friends. Well, I really think their goal should be learning to keep any of the friends that maybe they might already have. I can see why some of those kids in our group have a hard time with keeping friendships. Those stupid heads just say and do whatever! I try to just stay out of their way, so maybe I won't get noticed by them so much because I think they'll pick on me.

When it was my turn to talk about my friends, someone whispered, "He doesn't have any." Dr. Nick sent that kid who said that out of his office for two minutes for being mean. The counselor told me I was doing great and to please tell him what I'd like to do most with my best friend if anything was possible. Like, if we could go anywhere and do anything for free! Even the stupid heads wanted to answer that question, but I got to answer it first!

For activity today, Dr. Nick told us about a new game. He said the name of the game is "Good Choice", and the goal of the game is to make good choices whenever it's going to be our turn. Winners would be figured out by how good their choices were during the game.

The game board we used looked like an old checkerboard. The game had a starting point in the middle of the board, but it didn't have a spot to end or finish. It was kind of cool but weird too. Us kids were given a little game piece to use and could move it in any direction we wanted to, depending on the number we rolled on the dice. I think the only limits in the game were about how much time we'd get and the choices we got to make.

Today, the counselor had set and hid a timer to go off while we were playing, but he didn't tell anybody when that would be. We rolled just that one dice to see who would go first. The highest number rolled would get to go first, and we would go in a circle after that.

No matter what square you picked to land on, you had to answer a question from Dr. Nick. The counselor said that most of our questions were going to be about things that happen in life, and life answers usually need to be explained.

Some examples of the questions that were asked during the game were:

On your way to becoming a preacher, you found a five dollar bill on the playground and you thought it belonged to a friend of yours. What would you do and why?

On your way to becoming a sports star, you saw one of your friends take another friend's lunch. What would you do?

On your way to becoming a martial arts teacher, your cousin is selling drugs and your school's D.A.R.E. officer asks you, "Do you know anyone that sells drugs?" What would you say?

On your way to becoming the best dad in the world, your mother told your father she stopped smoking cigarettes, but you had seen her smoking since then. How would you handle that situation?

On your way to becoming a group leader, if someone offered you a hundred and eight dollars for pushing a button in a computer room on an island and you wouldn't know what would happen, what would you do?

On your way to becoming a doctor, name your top five priorities or most important things in life?

On your way to becoming the world's greatest mom, what do you believe happens to a person once they die?

On your way to becoming a plumber, would you rather have fifty thousand dollars right now or ten good years added on to the end of your life?

On your way to becoming a school principal, if it were possible for you to call and talk for ten minutes on the phone to someone you had known who had passed away, who would it be and what might you talk about?

On your way to becoming a movie star, if you had to go through life with just one of these things as your greatest strength, which would you choose: great looks, extreme intelligence, or a super personality? Keep in mind that even though the one thing you choose will be very strong, the two things you don't choose will be very, very weak.

Some of the questions Dr. Nick had asked were way hard to answer. Kids used the words depends and well lots of times.

I was really having fun listening to and answering the questions, even though I was told not to shout out answers to questions that weren't mine. Dr. Nick did let everyone answer the questions he asked once the player whose turn it was answered first.

It was weird playing the game because even though we moved our game pieces, you didn't know where to go. That one stupid head who has zero friends said, "How am I supposed to beat anybody if I don't know where I'm supposed to go?" The only thing Dr. Nick said was, "Matt, you only have a hidden timer and your very best answers to help you figure out how well you're doing. Be sure to do your best at all times."

That didn't help much.

We played the game until the timer went off. Time seemed to go by pretty fast, and everyone got to answer at least four or five questions. Lots of us wanted to keep playing and asked for more time, but the counselor said, "You get what you get, and you don't throw a fit." I didn't really like his answer, but I remembered that's exactly what I say sometimes too!

The counselor went over some of our answers we had given during the game. I liked that he had written down some of what I said. I guess it made me feel pretty important. He told me I did a really good job thinking about my answers before I said them. Dr. Nick told everybody that doing our best answering really hard questions does matter even if it's not our turn!

Dr. Nick said there are some things in life that just happen when they're supposed to happen. No one knows for sure when or why they do and that they're usually really hard, if not sometimes impossible, to explain. He told us he wants us to always do our best no matter what happens or what direction we seem to be headed in.

He also said that becoming something is just as important as being that something. I'm not for sure what he said, but he did explain what he meant. Dr. Nick said we're all going to have really important jobs when we get older, things like being teachers, doctors, firemen, friends, ministers, sport stars, dads, and moms. Now here's the part that I didn't get the first time. He said the decisions we make while we're becoming those things will be just as important to us as the ones we make once we become those things. I was kinda getting what he was saying but not really yet.

The counselor talked to the kid in our group who had the goal of keeping friends. Dr. Nick told him, "The decisions you make about your friendships is just as important as the decisions you made in wanting to become a friend. Like, if a good friend found his buddy's lost five dollar bill on the playground, he would definitely give it back." Now I got it! I guess my answers weren't the only answers the counselor had kept track of!

We went over some more of those questions he asked us about earlier and every time we did, Dr. Nick kept talking about decisions we make along the way being important. A couple of times I think, Dr. Nick would look at me a little bit but say stuff to everybody about making smart and active decisions now so we don't become victims or targets for bullies later when we're grown up.

Dr. Nick let us keep our game pieces as a reminder of what we learned in counseling today. He said he thinks we should talk to our families and friends about the easy and hard questions we try to figure out every day before time runs out.

Dear Parent,

Your child participated in a group counseling session today. Check-in provided boys and girls the opportunity to talk about their successes with family, school, and friends. Today's counseling activity was formatted in a game that involved the use of a checkerboard and a handful of questions. The purpose of the game was to help your child understand that no matter what he or she wants to "become" as a grown-up, character development is a daily and on-going process; one which really decides what we become.

GOING THROUGH YUCK

Goal of Activity: In this activity the student will experience the positive results of having applied determination and perseverance in times of uncertainty and hardship.

Student Mix: boys and girls of similar age and grade.

Group Size: four to six students

Suggested Time: thirty to forty minutes

Materials Required: large bucket of yuck, polished stones, paper towels, and awards

Considerations:

Most boys and girls will go through some really difficult times in their lives. Finding a way to help them understand that no matter what the yuck in their lives may be, they will not only get through it, but will ultimately prosper because of their efforts. Remember, for many kids counseling is the vehicle that helps transport them out of yucky memories, yucky relationships, and yucky environments to a healthy and happier place. As a counselor, you must remember that as a facilitator of change, seldom do we have a rocket ship or time machine to get kids where they need to go.

Instead, sometimes the best we can do is just keep them moving along in the right direction, even if it's at a snail's pace.

Any non-toxic, non-corrosive substance will work well in this activity. Personally, I prefer a mixture of colored gelatin and noodles. Keep it in the refrigerator as long as possible. If you happen to be running several groups that day, it's a good idea to have more than one bucket of yuck available. You could also use hot water and uncooked macaroni noodles to create another unforgettable sensation.

To add some additional suspense, consider covering the bucket of yuck with a darkened trash liner. The student's reaction of going through yuck without having the ability of actually seeing what they're going through is priceless. Be prepared, however, to provide encouragement in the form of reassurance and support to students who may show visible signs of ambivalence. The desire to find the one good thing, yet having to go through the unknown to find it, will increase some student's anxiety and raise past or present issues. Keep in mind, however, that from a counseling perspective students are frequently unable to give a name to the yuck they are experiencing in life, let alone understand it. All the kids are really left to deal with is all the yucky feelings they have. This is where you come in.

Student Reflection:

I had counseling group today with our school counselor. We began counseling group with something Dr. Nick calls check-in. Check-in is the time everyone in our group gets to say something important about family, school, and friends. Today he even asked that we share our three favorite movies or books.

Usually I don't say too much during check-in, but today I said a lot about my favorite movies. I was surprised and really pretty excited hearing that a couple other kids in group like the same movies I do.

While we were doing check-in, our counselor asked that we talk about a family member, a friend, and a teacher who we really appreciate. He said appreciate means like being valuable to us.

One of the kids in our group talked about his step dad and how he's glad his step dad treats him like his own kid. I know all about that. This girl talked about her friendship with a next door neighbor. She said that this is the neighbor who brings her to school on the days her mom either works the graveyard shift or stays overnight at her boyfriend's house.

Sometimes I'm not sure how I should act or what I should say when I hear things like that. It helps when the counselor reminds us to be respectful and supportive of each other.

Once everyone did check-in, we got to do the counseling activity. Dr. Nick told us he was going to test our perseverance and determination. Like I knew what that meant! It sounded good, but I had no idea what he just said. I think he likes to surprise us with big words sometimes because of the way we look at him and say, "What?"

He explained that determination is a lot like wanting something more than anything else, and that perseverance is making the effort to get that something. Dr. Nick gave the example of wanting an apple on a tree and then climbing the tree to get the apple. Now that made sense!

He put a bucket on top of the table we were sitting at. The bucket was filled with yucky stuff that looked like...I don't know what! We weren't really sure what the stuff was made of, and we couldn't get him to tell us what the gunk was either.

Dr. Nick told us to roll up our sleeves and then gave us two choices. We could reach in the bucket one at a time and feel around for a valuable stone that we could keep forever and ever. Or we could hold a friends hand while we reach in the bucket to help find the valuable stone, and we would still get to keep it forever and ever.

He said we might have to look for a very long time but promised us that each of us would find something really worthwhile and very valuable. I got the feeling this was going to be gross, but I was also very, very excited!

All the kids, except this one girl, took turns and reached into this grossest bucket of crap! You should have seen the looks on their faces as they wiggled through the bucket with nothing but their bare hands! I won't forget how I felt. I was feeling so nervous and excited that I almost wet my pants! Still, I liked having the other kids watch me as I watched them look at me! I hope they didn't notice my pants though.

Dr. Nick had to sit right by Mercedes and had to keep telling her it was going to be okay and for sure she would find something good in the yuck if she would just do it. Everybody who searched the bucket of yuck did, just like the counselor said, found a diamond, emerald, or ruby! Well, that's what Dr. Nick called them. I think maybe they were really just shiny rocks.

Dr. Nick had a towel for everyone to clean up with. He congratulated each of us and told us we could turn our stones in for a real prize. He also gave us an award to wear on our shirts. All the ribbons said "Determination and Perseverance" on them.

After we got cleaned up a little bit, Dr. Nick talked with us about how everybody has to go through some yucky stuff, just like the bucket of yuck we were in today. He promised us that if we keep searching for the one thing that will make all the yuck worthwhile, we would find it.

When he said that the yuck for some kids might be a family divorce, death of somebody we love, or even sometimes when a family has to go without money, I knew what he was talking about. He was sort of talking about the bucket of yuck, but he was also talking about yucky things that happen to kids too.

Some kids got talking about some of the yucky things they have already gone through. Dr. Nick reminded the girl sitting across from me how her one sister is needing a heart operation and how her whole family is going through some tough or yucky times.

One guy said he's going through some yucky times right now because his mom is going to court, and he may not get to see her for a while. My one friend who didn't stick her hand in the bucket wasn't talking. Dr. Nick asked her to say something, anything at all, but she just stayed quiet.

Our counselor said that hanging in there or searching through the yuck might take minutes, days, months, or even years to find that one thing that makes all the yucky stuff we've gone through worthwhile. He also said that if we don't hang in there and look, then we'll never find it anyway.

In doing the bucket of yuck stuff, it only took each of us a few seconds, which kinda seemed like it took a lot longer, to find a prize. Dr. Nick promised everybody, especially the girl who didn't do the activity, that everything would be okay as long as she kept searching for that one good thing, and he was here to help her find it. He said, "That's why you can choose a friend to help you go through yucky stuff."

I thought it was pretty cool that he gave her a really shiny diamond and told the girl that if she ever wants to, she can find her own treasure or ask a friend for help to find one. I think he also told her she could come back at lunch and talk about what she wants her diamond to be.

Dr. Nick said we could keep the treasure we found as a way to remember what our activity was really about. He also said that even though our friends, family, and teachers can't find the treasure for us, they will help us look for it if we just ask them to.

Dear Parent,
During the day, your child attended a counseling session. The activity required your child to reach into a bucket of "yuck" in search of a valuable ruby, emerald, or diamond. What the lesson really taught was how most kids have to go through some "yucky" things in their lives. However, no matter if the "yuck" is death, divorce, or parental incarceration, learning to be patient and persistent in finding something good even in the "yuckiest of times" will be the most valuable treasure of all.

ROCK AND SOCK ROBOTS

Goal of Activity: To promote the concept of non-violence, encourage and practice non-violent behavior, and to reward students for demonstrating safe and reasonable behavior in the midst of conflict.

Student Mix: students of similar age and grade; gender mixing not advised

Group Size: four to six students

Suggested Time: thirty to forty minutes

Materials Required: robotic fighters, tape recorder, whistle, index cards, and jaw breaker candies

Considerations:

The robots make this activity fun, the comments the boys and girls generate make it real, and we have to make it mean something. Helping a student learn how to walk away from a potential fight is what every teacher, principal, good parent, and counselor want. Remember, walking or running away to safety is often the most frequently underused option of self-defense. We can always review the underlying issues prompting an act of potential violence at a later and safer time for everyone involved.

Be selective as you collect your list of fighting names and gestures for the kids to use. Having a student go home and tell his or her parents that the counselor taught him a new word may not necessarily be a good thing.

Consider using the tape recorder to only record and playback the sounds of the kids being successful. That is, avoid recording the student picking a fight with his or her peer. Depending upon the student and how well you present the lesson, you don't want to inadvertently praise a behavior you are trying to extinguish. It's a wonderful feeling, however, for the student to hear over and over again the positive acknowledgment he receives from his peers for doing the right thing.

Student Reflection:

I met in counseling group today with Dr. Nick and the other kids. He had a bowl of treats we could choose from when we came in, just for coming to group. We could earn another cookie or something if our behavior in counseling group was what Dr. Nick said was appropriate.

I think he knew that some of us didn't know for sure what appropriate meant, so instead of him trying to explain what the word meant, he asked us to give him examples of reasonable, polite, and safe behaviors. Being a good listener, waiting your turn, wearing a seatbelt, walking away from trouble, and not kicking someone under the table while he was talking, were some of the examples that we all came up with. Dr. Nick said that's exactly what appropriate behavior is all about!

We started group with check-in. During check-in everyone gets to say something important about family, school, and friendships. When the time came to talk about school, Dr. Nick asked if we were on time, turning in our assignments, and staying out of trouble. Most of us were doing a pretty good job. With one or two kids, the counselor reminded those guys to MYOB. I remember the day we did that activity! Dr. Nick said he really liked our honesty and that he also likes to talk with our teachers so he can hear how great we're doing too.

In getting ready for our counseling activity, Dr. Nick had our group come up with a list of reasons why people might get into a fight. Everyone said a lot of things, and our answers were written on the whiteboard. This list was going to be called our list of fighting words.

When we got done, our list had name calling, eye rolling, flipping someone off, getting into somebody's face, spreading rumors, and trash talk that went from bad words about family members to teasing someone about how they look and smell.

I felt embarrassed but in an excited way when the counselor asked for examples of what we meant about bad things about family. I looked around the room to see who might say or do something first when suddenly, I heard the kid next to me say, "Your Momma!" I looked at Dr. Nick to see if he was getting mad and if the boy who said it was going to get into trouble. I was really surprised when the counselor calmly said, "Is that the best you've got?"

One at a time, Dr. Nick gave each of us a turn to give an example or sample of how to start a fight. I thought for sure we were all going to get in trouble, but we never did. My dad would kick my butt and ground me for a week if he heard me say any of those things and not back them up! The counselor did tell us though that this was part of our activity, and we should always try to avoid acting disrespectfully and saying such unkind things.

Once our list was done, I wasn't surprised that guys like me don't like to be called names like, "Wannabe, Punk, and Pervert." We also didn't like it if another guy walked up to us and suddenly threw his arms up in the air as if saying, "Come on!"

Girls got way mad with names like, "Stuffer, Hoochy, and Unibrow." The girls in our group for sure didn't like being called the

"B" word or having anyone talk smack about their moms or who their daddy is.

Dr. Nick had us think of ideas on what a fighting student would gain and lose if that kid got into a fight. He helped us come up with things like reputation, respect, privileges, and how we feel about ourselves.

I thought it was way too cool when our counselor placed his set of conflict managers on our table. Actually, they looked like Rock'em - Sock'em Robots. He said we were going to be using the robot fighters during our activity!

He had us choose anybody else in group to start a fight with. Too cool! A couple of kids right away began wrestling around as if they were wrestlers and kickboxers. I then heard this really loud whistle! Dr. Nick had blown the whistle to stop the kids. I think he knew this might happen. Dr. Nick explained we'd be using the robots to be doing the fighting for us. He said the person who was going to start the fight could only use one of the samples from the whiteboard. Everybody was pushing each other to see who would go first.

After like a five-minute time out, we got started again. It was kind of weird and funny to hear mean things being said in front of a grown-up. It was also pretty weird to hear kids make themselves say mean things when they were just pretending to be mad. Lots of us couldn't stop laughing because it was kind of embarrassing.

When it was my turn to start a fight, I said, "Hey, stupid, at least I have friends!" We were ready to fight! I was in control of one robot fighter, and my friend was in control of the other robot. We were supposed to knock the block off of the other guy's fighter before our robot had his head knocked off.

I was surprised that a couple kids in our group really got

into just watching the two fighters go at it. People were actually cheering and booing the robots! It was really getting loud!

Everyone was able to fight one another at least once before Dr. Nick had us come back together around the table and try the activity again without the robots and without the fighting. We took turns picking fights with each other using the words or gestures from the whiteboard, but this time we practiced walking away from the person trying to start a fight.

The kids in group who weren't doing anything but standing around and watching were told to congratulate and be supportive of the kid who had walked away from the area. We practiced doing this a couple times, and each time I got better at walking away. I liked hearing from the other kids how well I did. I usually don't hear that. I was remembering how my dad tells me to always hit somebody if they start any crap with me. I don't think I'll tell him about this activity.

Once everyone had practiced walking away, we talked about how using the robots to fight didn't really settle anything. Basically, it seemed like fighting only made the whole problem worse. That's when Dr. Nick let us hear the recording tape he had taken of us fighting! I felt embarrassed and kinda ashamed of myself when I heard the words I used to start a fight with my friend. I also felt embarrassed when I heard my voice above the other voices on the tape cheering for one of my friends to beat the crap out of this other kid in group. I sounded just like my dad.

I felt much better when the counselor played the tape of us walking away from the fight. I really liked hearing how my friends supported me in doing the right thing. I like feeling good about myself and feeling like I did the right thing.

When we left group, Dr. Nick gave everyone a jaw breaker candy and a card that read, "Violence is a bully that can show up any place, any time, and only smart and peaceful behavior can make him leave."

Dear Parent,

In counseling group today, your child participated in an activity that encouraged the use of "walking away" from potential violence with peers. Group members had the opportunity to role play various situations that typically provoke a fighting response in some boys and girls. Unlike the robotic fighters that had their "blocks knocked off," the kids in group were rewarded and praised for their decisions to walk away from violence and all the hardships that violence can bring.

SAILING

Goal of Activity: To promote decision-making skills that encourage and reward greater than self thinking.

Student Mix: boys and girls of similar age and grade

Group Size: five students

Suggested Time: thirty to forty minutes

Materials Required: large sheets of colored paper, regular paper, pencils, banners, and salt water taffy

Considerations:

Most girls and boys have no problem seeing themselves as the star of their own story. Being the star, they expect star treatment. Unfortunately, when children fail to transition out of this stage a larger than life sense of entitlement may begin to emerge. Helping a student learn how to think of him/herself as just one important part of a larger more important story is what this lesson is all about. This activity can be both fun and insightful. As a counselor you will enjoy seeing how the kids problem solve and come to the decisions they reach.

Some of the more bossy kids will want to direct how things happen, while other students may meekly accept the directives given. Take this as one of your first clues as to who is expecting star treatment.

Be careful to temper your involvement in their process of cargo/ship elimination. Kids also need to learn how to live with the choices they make regardless of whether they are the ones making or accepting the terms. This is also an important concept you may want to process with the group sometime toward the end of the session.

Student Reflection:

I went to counseling today. Dr. Nick met each of us at the door as we walked into his room, and he told us that he liked the way we got there without killing each other.

The room was set up just like it usually is, but today there were six chairs around the table, counting Dr. Nick's. We started counseling with check-in, which meant everybody had to talk about family, school, and friendship stuff.

I had decided that I was going to say something about my family today. Normally, I don't like saying too much because I feel like the other kids might think I'm goofy or weird. By now though, I know everyone has weird families and besides, Dr. Nick treats us all the same and seems to like everybody just the same too.

I took a big breath and tried to talk, but nothing came out except water from my nose and my eyes. Everybody got quiet and then asked me what was wrong. I talked about how my parents are going to be living in two different houses. I also told everyone that I don't like knowing I won't be able to see my mom and dad together. I stopped talking then because I felt like crying more.

It felt really good when the kids in group told me everything would be all right, and Dr. Nick looked at me and told me I would always make the right decisions when it comes to what's best for my family. Waiting so long to finally say something about what I was thinking probably wasn't so great, but I guess I was just more ready today. It helped that Dr. Nick told me today was the perfect day for having told him that and he thanked me for choosing just the right time to say it.

Once we all got done doing check-in, Dr. Nick showed us the stuff he had written on the whiteboard before we all got there.

Name one of your favorite foods that would be hard to go without.

What kind of drink would you really miss if you couldn't have it anymore?

As part of a five-person team, if you had to be one of the team's senses, like the eyes, ears, nose, mouth, or hands, which one would you be?

If you had to keep your friend away from a really fun place that he/she loves because you know it's bad for him/her, how would you do that?

As the last kid in our group told what he'd do and stuff, Dr. Nick handed out a large sheet of colored paper to everybody for our counseling activity. The counselor said we were going on a make-believe journey using a ship, and we were going to use the paper to make part of our uniform. With the colored sheet of paper, Dr. Nick showed us how to make captains' hats. We were going to become sailors!

Once our hats were made, he gave each of us a small banner that had a word on it. Everyone had a different word. The words were: foods, personals, clothing, luxuries, and tools. Dr. Nick explained through definitions and examples what the words meant.

Some of us noticed that the color of our banners matched the color of our hats. Pretty cool!

As captain of our own ship, each of us had been asked to make a list of five items (cargo) that went with our banner. For example, I was captain of the food ship, I got to choose any five food things I wanted, like pizza, pears, nachos, soda, and candy, to load on my ship. All the other captains got to do the same thing like I did but just with their stuff.

After our lists were done, our list of stuff got put up on the whiteboard under our banners. Our counselor then made this big announcement to put on our captains' hats and that our fleet of ships would sail together to unknown lands to begin a new town!

Things got kinda weird after we got going. For whatever reasons, we had to start to get rid of some of our stuff. Like, one time Dr. Nick said, "Your ship is too heavy and will sink if you don't get rid of part of your cargo." Another time he said, "Part of your cargo has been infected by rats. Choose one group of your remaining things to throw overboard." Every ship captain made his own decision about what cargo to keep and what stuff got to be tossed overboard.

I thought my choice was pretty good. I chose to dump my boxes of nachos and pizza. Everybody else thought I was crazy because they said I should have gotten rid my boxes of pears first! I love pears, and nobody was going to tell me what to do but it also made me feel like I didn't know what to do. Everybody else had to make choices just like I did, and Dr. Nick heard all of them and didn't tell us what to do.

Just when we were about to get to where we were supposed to be going, Dr. Nick told us some not so good news. He said that there was only parking space in the harbor for four ships. One of our ships and all of its stuff, but not its captain, would have to be left behind. Dr. Nick gave us two minutes to talk it over and make that decision.

Everybody pointed fingers at everybody else. Finally, pretty much everybody except this one girl agreed that one of our ships was going to be left behind. Somebody said it was going to be turned into a submarine. That was funny!

The girl who was captaining that submarine ship got really, really mad, and I guess didn't think it was so funny. She called everybody stupid. It was good that Dr. Nick told her it would probably be best that it worked out this way for everybody. I guess she was really upset because he had to keep telling her stuff like, "Don't take it personal," "It's for the good of everyone," and "You did the right thing." I think he was going to talk to her later too.

When we were done with that, Dr. Nick said to everybody that we did a very good job with planning, fixing our plan as we sailed, and made decisions that were in the best interest of everyone in our group, not just ourselves.

Dr. Nick then reminded us about some of the questions he had asked us just after check-in. He asked that we remember the questions about having to give up a favorite food and drink. He also said to remember the question about sharing our five senses as part of a team of other people. Like having one kid be the eyes, having another person be the ears, and then having someone else be the mouth. The last question he asked us to remember was the one about how to stop a friend from going someplace they love but we know that it's bad for them. I really didn't like those last two questions at all. Those were the toughest questions for me to answer for sure!

Our counselor said that sometimes even kids have to act like captains because we might have to make some really hard decisions that we don't like but they help the people we're with. He said, for example, maybe like having to leave behind a friendship with one person because everybody else in the family can't stand that person. Sometimes that choice might be about trying to like dad's new girlfriend because it makes him happy, and that seems to make everything go smoother.

Dr. Nick also told us how some people might have a bad relationship with things and not people like how if someone might be addicted to drugs, alcohol, gambling, or using the computer too much. The counselor said that people sometimes need to make hard decisions about leaving those bad relationships behind too because there wouldn't be room for the really important people in their lives. I knew what he was talking about now!

Bobby told Dr. Nick that one time he had to go to a movie that everyone else in his family wanted to see but not him. Then Myeisha, the girl whose ship was sunk and had called us all stupid, said she's having to share her bed with her two high school cousins even though she doesn't want to. She said her mom told her to stop being so selfish because her cousins need a bed too. Dr. Nick looked at her for a minute and then told her something like he was proud of her for not wanting to give up her need for privacy just to help everybody else. He also said he wanted to talk to her later by herself so he can better understand more about what's going on. He said that sometimes nobody should have to give up, throw away, or sacrifice some things that are really important, even if it makes things better for everybody else. That seemed to make her smile.

We talked for a little more about making good group decisions even though we don't always feel like it and maybe even because it's not what we want. Dr. Nick said that if I ever need to make a choice between staying at my mom's or dad's house, not to worry about it. He said I would get to see my parents together again but just not as much as I'm used to. Dr. Nick told me to be a captain and to think about what's best for everybody in my family, even if we're on two different ships. He told me again how proud he was of me for telling him about my family and that he would be a good listener whenever I wanted him to be.

Dr. Nick let us keep our hats, and we got to wear them back to class if we wanted to. He also gave everybody some salt water taffy and told us to be sure to always talk about hard decisions with our family, friends, and other people we know and trust.

Dear Parent,

If your child comes home with a sailor's hat on, it's probably because he or she was in counseling today! After introductions and check-in, students were assigned to be captains of their own ships. Every captain had to make some difficult decisions on a make-believe journey across the sea. Although your child was in charge of his or her own ship, all captains were considered members of the same fleet. Be sure to ask your child about the family lesson he or she learned along the way!

THE SECRET RECIPE

Goal of Activity: To help the student learn to identify the components of an enjoyable experience and to encourage the student to actively create successful experiences regardless of the situation he may be in.

Student Mix: boys and girls of approximately the same age and grade

Group Size: four to six students

Suggested Time: thirty to forty minutes

Materials Required: index recipe cards, pencils, and treats

Considerations:

Students can identify with recipes pretty well. Most have a recipe book at home and have probably seen at least one of their parents or grandparents using the book to cook from.

In this activity you want to instill the notion that certain things can be created, whether those things are baked goods, a party atmosphere, or even a Frankenstein monster. Once a student understands that concept, the rest of the activity becomes possible.

It's important that you try to draw upon enjoyable experiences the students have already experienced in formulating their list of special ingredients. Teaching students how to identify the thoughts and feelings that are at the heart of every enjoyable experience is the second step in learning how to create them. Helping and nurturing the students believe in their ability to create a positive experience is the first.

Student Reflection:

I met with Dr. Nick and the rest of the kids in my group for counseling today. We began group by going over our goals. This is, I think, like only my fifth or sixth time in counseling. I remember when I first started, Dr. Nick helped me come up with at least three goals. One goal was something about my family, and the other ones were about school and my friendships mostly with the kids at school.

My school goal is to get better at reading. The counselor helped me figure out how much reading I'll need to do every week to make my word goal by the end of the year. I also have a family goal of spending more time with my dad. Dr. Nick gave me a couple ideas on how to get my dad not to be so lazy and to do more things with me. Like one idea he said was to hide the remote control and all of my dad's beer. I think he was kidding but I wasn't sure. He said my dad would want me to help him look for those things and that would be kinda like doing stuff together!

Once everybody talked about their goals, we did a real quick check-in. Today in check-in I didn't feel like saying too much else. I really felt like just getting into the activity. I guess I wasn't the only one. Dr. Nick told us there would be no counseling activity unless everyone participated in check-in and that means saying more than, "Everything is fine." We all took time to talk about what's going on with our families, school, and friends, but we didn't really have to say so much because everybody had goals about those things.

During check-in, Dr. Nick had asked questions like, "Did anyone in your family celebrate a birthday this past week?" "Who in your family did you get along best with this past week?" "Which chores are you really good at?" and, "How is your day different when you're on time for school versus being late for school?"

I actually like doing check-in even though I don't always want to get into it. I really like knowing and having things pretty much be the same each time I come here. I won't say that out loud because no one else has.

Counseling activity got started with Dr. Nick asking us if we knew what a recipe is. I know I do! Recipes are pretty much the directions and ingredients used to make something like cookies, cakes, chili, or pizza. He then wanted us to tell everybody else about any of our favorite recipes.

I noticed that sugar goes into a lot of stuff. I love sugar, it makes me feel great! Dr. Nick said that some grown-ups love the stuff inside coffee and Mountain Dew because it makes them feel great for a little while too!

Our counselor told us he was going to teach us some new recipes, but these recipes aren't really used for cooking. Dr. Nick used the whiteboard to write down the names of some special types of ingredients that we would be using in our counseling activity today. The ingredients were stuff like: courage, patience, laughter, respect, kindness, happiness, faith, fun, companionship, sharing, optimism, and forgiveness. He then tried to explain what each word meant.

That seemed to take forever.

Dr. Nick then asked each one of us to talk about one of the best days we'd ever had, and I noticed he kept writing down stuff we said. I heard about some really great days for sure, like going to Disneyland, being on vacations, and doing lots of running around to different places with family and friends.

It was kind of funny that whenever somebody said something about one of his best memories, Dr. Nick would find a word on the whiteboard and say something like, "Oh, so this is what you're talking about."

After we all had talked about one of our best days, Dr. Nick said that no matter what we did or where we went, our best days came down to a bunch of thoughts and feelings we had. He pointed to the whiteboard where lots of those thoughts and feelings had been written into words that described them.

Dr. Nick gave each of us a special recipe card and asked that we write down our own secret recipe using some of the special ingredients we had on the whiteboard. He also said to remember how we felt on one of our best days, just like the one we had talked about earlier. The counselor said once we got that done, we were going to use our recipes to turn a not-so-good day into a good day for ourselves or someone else.

Our recipes had to total 100%, and they also had to have where we might use each ingredient. Like, a good day might be made up of this kind of stuff:

30% Laughter at home doing dishes.

20% Kindness at school waiting in lunch line.

30% Positive attitude during math.

20% Forgiveness with a friend who told a lie.

He gave everyone two or three recipe cards and told us to use a pencil in case we want to change our recipes or change our minds. That's good because I'm a pretty "krappy" speller.

I kinda knew what he wanted me to do, but I still wasn't quite sure exactly how he wanted me to do it. It helped that he drew a recipe card on the whiteboard and made us look at what he was doing.

He also said to think of the places where we might really need to have a good day. That place might be on a long car drive, waiting in a lunch line, or where the person sitting next to us is really being a pain or bothering us. Now I got it! He was talking about me sitting next to my sister on our family's drive to the farm in South Dakota. She can ruin anything!

Everyone worked really hard at coming up with recipes for turning a bad day into a good one. Once we finished, Dr. Nick had us talk about our recipes with one another until it was getting time to be going.

The counselor told everybody to think about using our recipe cards at least four times this week or whenever we feel our day is beginning to go bad. He said that we should share our secret recipe with family, friends, or anyone else who's having a bad day because that's why people share good recipes.

Dr. Nick gave everybody a Good and Plenty piece of candy and a blank recipe card today when we were leaving his office. He said he would ask us next time how we used our recipe cards during the week.

I told him I'm going to write a special recipe card to my dad that would have him doing 50% being at his work, 25% doing stuff with my mom, and 25% just hanging out with me not watching football or drinking beer. I'd also tell my dad that I love him 100% of all the time.

Dear Parent,

If your child had any previous experience baking cookies or adding the secret ingredient to the family chili, then he or she understood the counseling activity. The goal of the activity was to have students identify the "secret ingredients" of any good experience. Being kind, polite, helpful, and considerate were just a few of the secret ingredients used today. Students were then encouraged to use the recipe in helping themselves and others in turning a "not so good" day into a "good day" in the upcoming week.

INSIDE OUT

Goal of Activity: Students will develop a greater sense of self through the exploration of their own inner and outer qualities. Students will also be encouraged to see beneath the physical characteristics of others and recognize their own unique characteristics.

Student Mix: boys and girls of similar age and grade

Group Size: four to six students

Suggested Time: thirty-five to forty-five minutes

Materials Required: lunch-sized paper bags, crayons, colored pencils, markers, and plastic play glasses

Considerations:

Learning how to see more than just what a person looks like is really a difficult lesson to learn, largely because it's not easy to do and takes continuous practice. Several of the lessons in this book lend themselves toward accomplishing that goal, but this activity provides students with the best opportunity in expanding and magnifying the depth of their vision, regardless of their ages. If the sacks concept isn't successful, try introducing the activity with an envelope and an index card. Have the student draw a picture of him/herself on the envelope, then later insert his or her inner qualities card. Boys and girls will soon be amazed by their abilities in seeing beyond and beneath a person's exterior when the envelope is held in front of a lighted source!

Don't panic if you feel like you're spending too much time getting this activity set up. It's important that you not speed through the imagery segment. I think the success of the activity hinges on this component as it establishes the link between self-esteem and sustained effort.

Like many activities, it's easy for this lesson to go awry. Girls and boys have a unique and unexplainable gift for saying the things they do. Remember, you don't always have to comment on everything a student says. Sometimes it's best just to look at the student with a sense of understanding and nod your head to acknowledge what's been said. The art of taking and recalling mental notes will come in due time.

Student Reflection:

I got to be in counseling group today with our school counselor, Dr. Nick. I really like going to counseling group. I feel like I fit in pretty good there, mostly because I think he pays attention to me.

We did check-in, and everybody had to report on their goals. Like last time, Dr. Nick tried to get everyone to say something important about our week with family, school, and friends.

Today Dr. Nick was pretty curious about how we were doing in school. I couldn't tell for sure if he was curious, but he said he was. He also wanted us to put into order our subjects from most to least favorite. Like, if social studies was our favorite class that would be our first favorite. He kept track of our answers on the whiteboard. Not too many of the kids in our group like math so much. Science didn't do too well either because they were both last pretty much on everybody's list.

Even though I like reading and it was like my top thing, I sometimes get in trouble at school because I'm reading a book when the teacher thinks I'm supposed to be doing something else. I'm not bothering anybody so I don't get why my teacher throws a fit. Last time that happened, she sent me to the office for being defiant. That's crazy! I'm not defiant and that's what I told the teacher too!

When it was my turn during check-in, I thought about telling Dr. Nick about it so he could get her fired, but then I thought I didn't want to tell him about getting sent to the office either.

After check-in, Dr. Nick tried telling us why some kids just like doing the things they're good at, especially like the ones that don't take much effort. Like he said that some kids may just be really good at reading or gymnastics but choose not to really work at getting better at those things. Dr. Nick says that sometimes those types of kids might be called lazy or unmotivated by parents or teachers. He's right! I hate it when my mom calls me lazy. I get so mad I just won't do anything! That's not being lazy, that's just how I act when I get angry.

The counselor asked us to think about how we would feel if we tried really hard at something we're not so good at, like math, science, or even doing push-ups. Dr. Nick said if we work hard at something that doesn't come easy and show progress, we would feel really proud of what we've done, even though we've only improved just maybe a little bit.

Dr. Nick had us close our eyes and asked us to try and imagine what he was going to describe. Even though I didn't want to close my eyes the whole way, I pretended to keep them closed. This is what I heard him say:

> You are in a desert at the foot of a mountain of sand. From your view, the mountain seems to touch the sky. Your goal is to get as far up the mountain as possible, and you don't even like climbing! For every step you take, you seem to slide back two steps. Every step is hard and frustrating, but you stay

at it even though a part of you keeps calling this whole thing dumb and stupid.

Sweat is getting in your eyes, and it's really hard work. Eventually, you figure out how to make progress without sliding back down the mountain. Little by little you make progress. Every so often, you look over your shoulder to see how far you've come, then glance up to see how far you can go.

This is the moment you can really feel proud of yourself for coming as far as you have! You feel great because you didn't let that negative voice telling you it was dumb and stupid stop you. Remember, your goal was to make progress at something that was hard, and progress requires lots of effort.

When he asked us to open our eyes, he said everyone has a mountain to climb! We were all getting pretty excited because I thought he was going to take us some place on a school bus, like to a mountain or something. When he pointed to the whiteboard and said, "For some, that mountain might be math, science, or reading," I knew what he meant.

Dr. Nick told us that even if we're already really good at something, we still have that mountain to climb to really feel good about it. He told us about one of world's best basketball players. Dr. Nick said one of the reasons this guy is so great is because the player knew he had a lot of mountain left to climb even though he started out pretty high on the mountain to begin with. Like, he was better than most people without even trying hard. The more he practiced though, the higher he climbed, the higher he climbed, the better he became in basketball and felt even better about himself.

Dr. Nick encouraged each of us to work at making progress in our least favorite subject as well as one of our favorite sport skills. On a big sheet of paper he hung up, he wrote, "Feeling good about yourself doesn't end with where you start."

Finally we got our activity started! He gave everyone two small, brown paper bags, but one was inside the other. He also gave out some crayons and a few markers. Dr. Nick said we should use the crayons and markers to make the outside bag look like how we look to other people. I think he just wanted us to draw a picture of ourselves on the bag.

I'm not much of an artist unless we're drawing stick people, but I really had fun trying to make my picture look like me! One kid needed another bag because he messed up and got really ticked off! Dr. Nick told the kid that drawing might be one of his mountains to climb. What he told that kid made me think about what we talked about earlier, and I knew what he meant by that. One of my mountains might be drawing too, but I don't mind that so much. I want to get better at that.

Once our bags were done, Dr. Nick told us to take the inside sack out and write words on it that describe how we feel about ourselves. He also said we could write stuff we like to do, foods we like to eat, and movies we like to watch. For example, Dr. Nick had written on his bag: funny, clumsy, caring, anxious, and awkward. He also wrote the name of his favorite movie and that he likes playing pool. Some kids wrote words like: kind, funny, thoughtful, caring, generous, sensitive, athletic, worried, macho, active, nice, sweet, hopeful, anxious, optimistic, hot, lazy, and friendly. Dr. Nick had to remind us a few times not to use words that describe how we look but how we feel about ourselves. He said it didn't matter if those words were either good or bad ones, just be sure the words were about how we feel about ourselves.

When we finished doing our writing, the counselor asked us to place our word sack back inside the bag we had just drawn our own picture on.

What happened next was pretty neat. Dr. Nick lined the bags on the table in front of us and asked if we recognized each other. This was really pretty easy. I was the only stick figure with freckles out there!

Next is when things got definitely weird. Dr. Nick took the inside sacks out of their outer bags. He then mixed them all up. He put my inside sack into someone else's outer bag. He did that to everyone! For example, Vernon's inner sack ended up in Autumn's outer bag. That was just wrong!

He looked at each one of us in the group, pointed to our outer bag, and asked, "Is this you?" Well, that started lots of talking! We talked about who we are on the inside versus who we are on the outside. I think how I feel on the inside really tells more about who I am than how I look, but I'm pretty sure I'm both.

Like, I like being a boy. Vernon likes being a boy too. He insisted that he never feels pretty or feels like chasing boys. One girl in our group said she doesn't care how she looks as long as she feels good. She also said her mom likes girlfriends instead of boyfriends because they're more like her. Our counselor said not everyone feels the way they look. He also said just because you know how somebody looks doesn't mean you know how that person feels or what they're like.

For fun, Dr. Nick had us take turns reading the words inside our outer bag. So, for example, Vernon stood up and read the words written on the bag that Autumn had used to describe how she felt about herself! It was fun guessing who the words really described. I was pretty surprised to hear how some boys and girls feel about themselves, and I think Dr. Nick was surprised too because he kept writing down stuff about what everybody was saying.

Dr. Nick said it would be really cool if we could actually see how everyone sees themselves, but we would need a special kind of X-ray eyes to do that, eyes that see both the outside of how someone looks as well as how they feel about themselves on the inside. He said that learning to see others with X-ray vision might be just like climbing a mountain of sand for some of us. Hey! I knew exactly what he meant because we talked about that earlier!

As we left his office, Dr. Nick gave everyone both the inside and outside bags each of us had worked on in group. He also gave everyone a pair of plastic, black rimmed toy glasses with the words X-ray vision written on them.

He then reminded us of the sign he had made and placed on the wall earlier in group. He said to keep working hard at climbing that mountain that makes us see how people feel about themselves on the inside. When we can do that, said Dr. Nick, we'll feel really good about all of our progress too.

Dear Parent,

Your child was one of several students who seemed to enjoy group counseling today. After everyone had the chance to talk about family, school, and friendships; the students participated in a counseling activity. The activity was designed to help children identify and separate the inner and outer aspects of their identity. Paper sacks were used, one inside the other, to help visualize the concept of how two, sometimes very different, aspects of the same person come together.

JUMPING TO CONCLUSIONS

Goal of Activity: To encourage the student to learn how to pay attention to and accurately identify his or her feelings without jumping to conclusions.

Student Mix: boys and girls of similar age and grade

Group Size: four to six students

Suggested Time: thirty to forty minutes

Materials Required: paper, pencils, several tall containers, moistened paper towels, and treats

Considerations:

This is a fun activity in part to help determine how much self-control a student possesses. This is also a very exciting activity for students to participate in. It's been my observation that kids enjoy the attention they receive from the other students in group for just being themselves.

This is the type of activity that you must be prepared to repeatedly encourage the die hard attention seekers and the impulse control issue kids to refrain from blurting out their responses time after time. This activity is also a good instrument for improving self-control.

Many things can find their way into any of these boxes. As for what to put into your boxes, consider having combination textured surfaces as your first choice. For example, take a piece of wood and glue a section of sand paper on one of its sides. Filling a balloon up with water and gluing several cotton balls or feathers to it is also something to consider. By implementing a combination of textured surface items into a box or two, what you're really doing is helping kids concentrate on what they're feeling right now by not providing them with a jump to an easy conclusion opportunity or answer.

You may notice that by adding a little mystery and suspense to the activity, it's easy to therapeutically enhance a student's anxiety. Keep in mind, however, regardless of what you have or haven't placed in the box, know that uncertainty and apprehension fuel the imagination. This revealing of the student's symbolic and actual fears not only provides the counselor with a timely opportunity to offer credible reassurance, but also valuable insight into the student.

Student Reflection:

I felt really excited as I waited for the counselor to call me to counseling today. I know he's only here at our school one day a week, and he seems like he's always busy with a lot of kids. I was remembering him telling me that it was a good thing I had my mom sign my counseling permission slip, otherwise, I couldn't be in counseling. I was really glad I turned that paper in to my teacher to give to him so I wouldn't have to miss counseling again like last week. Dr. Nick told me I should be proud of myself for making sure I got all that stuff to happen.

When I got to group, we started off with introductions. We had a new girl join our group. Her name is Kaylee. She's from another state and moved here to live with her grandma. That's pretty much all she said, and Dr. Nick told her she did a great job.

For check-in, our counselor asked everyone the following

question, "Has there ever been a time when you were at home, in school, or with friends that you just didn't know what you were feeling and you really had a hard time figuring out what words to use to describe what you felt?"

I think I kind of knew what he was talking about, but I wasn't sure. I looked around the room to see if anyone else got what he was saying. Everybody looked like nobody understood what he said. That never stops Vivianna from blurting out any answer, even if she doesn't get the question, she likes being first in everything! Dr. Nick gave us a couple of his own examples to help us get what he was saying. His first example had something to do with the time he got this one phone call from the police to come down to the station to talk about some stuff. He said he was feeling nervous, scared, and worried, but that still didn't quite describe all he was feeling. He also told us about another time when he was a kid about our age and had been told by a teacher to stay after school to discuss his behavior. Now he said something about feeling worried, surprised, and anxious, but still, he wasn't sure. I think I was beginning to understand what he was asking us to think of now. Then when he said something about staying home alone at night and hearing different sounds, I really knew what he was talking about!

This one girl remembered a time she had heard loud voices coming from her mom's bedroom. She said that when she went into the room her mom and step dad suddenly stopped talking and did not talk again while she stayed there. She tried to describe how she felt, but the only words she could come up with were weird and scared. Lots of us talked about our own weird experiences. Even the new girl, Kaylee, said how she felt really weird when she left her mom to come live with her grandma.

After we finished getting done with doing check-in, Dr. Nick got us started on the counseling activity.

He showed us a tall and skinny box that he had put a sticker with the number one on it. The box reminded me of the kind that juice packets come in. Even though he wouldn't tell us what was in the box, he did promise that there was nothing inside the box that would cause skin damage if we touched it for a long time. Dr. Nick also really told us like five times not to guess out loud what we think the thing in the box is. Instead, he said our answer should be one that describes the feeling our hand is having.

We got to take turns to reach inside the box, feel whatever it was, and then write on a sheet of paper how the object felt. Dr. Nick then brought out more and more numbered boxes with things in them.

This was really getting to be very cool and exciting! Half the fun I had was just watching the faces of the kids as they put their hands inside the boxes. I'll never forget Brandon's face when he reached his arm inside one of the boxes! His eyes got really big and he yelled out, "Holy crap!" Dr. Nick had to tell everyone, lots of times, just to concentrate on how the objects feel and not be so quick to try and figure out what the things in the boxes are.

I'm pretty sure Dr. Nick had us put our hands in at least eight different boxes by the time we were done. He then had us read the word we used to describe how the item felt. Once everybody read their word, he brought the thing out from its box to show us what it was!

I was pretty surprised how good some of the kids did in de-scribing what they felt. Two kids were just way off and not even close with their descriptions. This one girl used the word "icky" for nearly everything. Even though Dr. Nick warned us not to, some kids had written the names of what they thought the things were.

Dr. Nick said that it's important to figure out what we're feel-ing, whether we've put our hand in a box or walked into a room full of people. He said that lots of boys and girls will jump to a conclusion about what's going on before even figuring out how they're feeling.

The counselor said that jumping to conclusions could cause some real problems, and he gave us an example of what he meant. He said like if we wanted to raise the temperature in our living room at home, we could throw more logs in the fireplace and turn the heater up really high. That might work a little bit but if we didn't first feel the cold air coming in from the open doors and windows, no matter how many logs we used, we couldn't get the room any hotter. Dr. Nick said that if we just kept throwing logs on the fire, we just might make the problem worse by creating a new problem, like the whole house catching on fire! That scared me, and we don't even have a fireplace at my house!

The counselor checked over some of our answers from check-in. He asked that one girl sitting next to me to guess what she thought was going on between her parents when she walked into their room. She said, "I thought they were talking about getting a divorce, and it made me feel really weird." Dr. Nick said that sometimes weird can be a mix of feelings like curiosity, confusion, and nervousness.

The girl was still listening pretty good because I could tell she was looking right at the counselor. When he asked her if her parents were actually going to get a divorce, she said: "No, my parents were trying to surprise me with planning a family vacation to Hawaii, but when they saw how upset I was, they just came out and told me." Man! Was she way off!

Dr. Nick also said he noticed that some of us seemed like we were pretty scared or nervous about reaching into some of the boxes and feeling around. No kidding! I thought maybe there was like a biting snake or a gross dead animal inside! He said that our imaginations are way more powerful than anything he could have put in any of the boxes, and that's why it's so important to figure out what we're really feeling first.

It seemed like group lasted almost forever today, but I was glad I came again. The counselor gave everybody a treat when we left his office, plus he had this one cardboard box lid lying down at the bottom of the step. He had wrote on the box lid, "Conclusions...don't jump in here."

Dear Parent,

Students often have a difficult time accurately identifying their feelings when something isn't quite right. Most kids have a tendency to "jump to a conclusion." Children often believe the sooner they give that something wrong a name, the sooner it can be fixed. Sound familiar? Today's counseling activity allowed kids the opportunity to concentrate only on describing what they felt. It's amazing how far our first "jump to a conclusion" can take us away from the reality of what we're actually feeling.

BUILDING FRIENDSHIP

Goal of Activity: To help the student understand the importance of trust in building relationships. The activity also helps boys and girls develop skills that foster good friendships.

Student Mix: boys and girls of approximately the same age and grade

Group Size: four to six students

Suggested Time: thirty to forty minutes

Materials Required: checkers, wood block, soft sponge block, and plenty of million dollar bills

Considerations:

Trust is a great thing, and not being able to trust a person you care about is devastating. Many of the boys and girls in counseling will have learned this lesson early in life by firsthand experience. As a counselor, use of this activity allows the opportunity to address an issue that many students prefer to remain silent about and avoid whenever they sense it coming.

In this activity, it's not unusual for girls and boys to simply assume this is a competition between groups in checker stacking. Let them believe that as long as you can, until you show them the bottoms of the bases. In terms of stacking checkers, allowing kids the opportunity to revel in the feelings of being successful and temporarily experiencing the feelings of frustration or disappointment is actually helpful in promoting a positive outcome in this activity. You must, however, be sure to connect their respective experiences of success to trust and validate their disappointment of having been let down.

During the course of the activity, try to figure out a way to teach your group members how to trust others in progressive moderation as time and exposure to potential friends permit. Think in terms of one checker at a time. Remember, this is going to be an ongoing process for students to work through and develop. This lesson has tremendous potential for aiding boys and girls in developing their skills in learning what friendships are all about.

Student Reflection:

I was in counseling group today with our school counselor, Dr. Nick. When he called my classroom, I was ready to run out the door. I felt so mad though when my teacher told me I had to finish taking my spelling test before I could go! When I finally got to Dr. Nick's office, I tried to explain why I was so late. He told me not to worry about it and that school work needs to come first. Besides, he said, "I know you trust your teacher to do the right thing."

I missed check-in, but I did get there just in time to answer a couple questions. One question Dr. Nick asked was, "What do you get out of counseling?" I told him, "I try to get out of spelling. Sometimes it works and sometimes it doesn't." Everyone seemed to like my answer because they all laughed. I guess though, that wasn't the type of answer Dr. Nick was thinking about. He laughed some and said, "What I meant was, what good do you get out of counseling?" Everybody had something to say, but I still think my answer was the best.

Dr. Nick had us think about our goals that each of us came up with when we first started in counseling. He said that, if nothing else, counseling is helping us reach our goals. He added that he also wants us to get something good out of counseling, whether it be a piece of candy, a good experience, or learn something that can help us later.

The other question Dr. Nick had asked was, "If you needed to trust one of your friends with a million dollars, who would it be and why?" Everyone but this one girl told our counselor who their million dollar friend was. That one girl who didn't have an answer said something about not having a good enough friend to trust, especially after what happened this weekend. That's all she would say about it.

Dr. Nick began our counseling activity by getting out two sets of building things. The sets were made up of about twenty checkers and something to build them on. Both sets of building things looked pretty much the same except for their bottom parts. One base was made of wood, about the size of my dad's wallet. The other base was about the same size, but it looked like it was made of sponge or foam or something.

The counselor split our group into two smaller groups. One group was told to stack their checkers on the piece of wood, and the other group had to stack their checkers on this foamy thing. We had to take turns, and Dr. Nick said he wanted to know which team was better at stacking checkers.

When we all first got started, both teams were doing pretty good. Pretty soon after like about eight checkers, my team's checkers would always fall over! We got to try to stack them again, but no matter how many times we did, our checkers would always fall over about after eight or nine checkers. Stupid game!!! I wanted to quit, but Dr. Nick told me and the other kids on my team to be patient.

We then got to trade our sets of building materials with the other team. This time my team had the block of wood and the red checkers. It was way better! We built our checkers way higher than the other team! I was glad to see them get mad and fail just like we had done. Now it was my turn to laugh and point my finger at them and remind them of how much of a group of losers they are!

Dr. Nick said something about being nice and humble, but I really liked laughing at the other kids' falling checkers. I even jumped up from my chair and did the "shimmy" to tease the other team because we were doing so good. About then, Dr. Nick gave me a pretty hard stare and reminded everyone about the treat to be earned at the end of group for kids being good sports and having shown respectful behavior. I was about to say something else, but he told me to be quiet and sit down.

Dr. Nick turned the piece of wood over, and written on the bottom of it was the word trust. There was also the math symbol ">," which means greater than. He then turned the foam bottom over, and it had the word trust on it too. The only difference I saw was that it had the math sign "<," which means less than.

He said that's why we could build checkers higher on the wood. Well, that didn't make any sense to me at all. I told him the reason was because the wood is more stronger than the sponge, and he told me that's exactly what he meant too! Dr. Nick said that good friendships are always built on trust. Like the greater or more stronger the amounts of trust in a relationship are, the stronger, better, and higher that friendship can go.

Our counselor had us imagine that the wood was a solid block of trust. He said that's why we could stack our checkers so high on the wood base. Wood is strong, sturdy, and very solid. He also told us to imagine the foamy thing being made up of questions, doubt, and worry. He explained the reason we couldn't stack our checkers very high on sponge was because friendship needs a solid base to build on and not stuff that won't hold up.

Dr. Nick had us do the stacking checker activity two more times to help us better understand about how important trust is. He asked that we think about our million dollar friend from check-in as we stacked checkers on the wood base. He told us to remember all the times our friends had kept their word, was there for us when we needed them, and could be counted on for keeping our private thoughts to themselves.

That was pretty good. Now all of us got to be on the same team, and we were able to get our checkers stacked really high on the wood base. We used all the checkers he had given us, and Dr. Nick said we broke the record! He then gave us the foamy thing to build on. He asked that we think about some of the people we know that we wouldn't trust with a million dollars, like a former friend or even certain family members. As we took turns and stacked checkers on the foam, Dr. Nick told us to remember that no matter how hard or careful we are, our friendships can't go any higher than the trust we have in that other person and that person's trust in us. He was right! As soon as he said that, our checkers fell over!

Some of the kids told Dr. Nick about some of the things that made them sad or angry with ex-friends or people in their families. The one girl who didn't have a million dollar friend said something like now having supervised visits with her dad. I think Dr. Nick was going to talk to her privately because he started to tell the girl they would talk about that stuff later.

Dr. Nick reminded us that even though we may have lots in common with friends like classes, favorite books, music, movies, and family stuff, to always remember how important trust is if we want to make "million dollar" friends.

While we were getting out of group today, Dr. Nick gave everybody a really big million dollar bill and told us to be smart when it comes to trusting it with our different friends and family members. He told us to make two lists of names of people. One list would be names of people we'd loan a million dollars to, and the other list would have names of people we wouldn't loan the money to. He said to keep the list pretty private and that he would like to look at it the next time we came.

Dear Parent,

Have you ever tried to stack blocks on a sponge? How about on a block of wood? Well, that's exactly what your child did in counseling group today. The counseling activity was designed to help your child understand that the basis of any good friendship is a strong foundation made of trust. Sometimes, fair weather friendships develop on things other than trust. One example is when kids find themselves getting taken advantage of for the things they have. Good friends want what's best for their friends, not themselves.

BALLOONS

Goal of Activity: To empower students to believe in their own abilities to replace passive worrying with the development of an active plan to succeed.

Student Mix: boys and girls of similar age and grade

Group Size: six to eight students

Suggested Time: thirty-five to forty-five minutes

Materials Required: helium container, balloons, string, paper, pencils, soft-tipped markers, cardboard cut-out figure, little round stickers, and treats

Considerations:

I've come to believe that most girls and boys handle worry in one of two ways. First, there are the students who wear the look of worry. You can tell something is wrong with these children just by the expression of uncertainty they wear on their faces. Think of bunny rabbits about to cry.

At the other end of this spectrum are the boys and girls who look blunted. Blunted in the sense of having a flat affect, limited expression, and what might be considered as having a monotone demeanor. Don't forget angry. I think some blunted looking students have been exposed to uncertainty for so long that they've adopted the belief that nothing matters, along with an "I don't care" response to most things. Tragically, they've quit getting their hopes up a long time ago.

Students potentially have many things to worry about. Anything and everything from who they'll play with at recess and sit with at lunch, to how they're getting home from school and where they will be sleeping to-night. When you help a student to replace worry with a reasonable plan of action, you have empowered the student to become a vital part of his or her own solution rather than a victim of circumstance.

Student Reflection:

I got to be in counseling group today. It's pretty neat that Dr. Nick gave everyone a treat just for coming to group! He said he really likes that we spend part of our day with him and that he likes having the chance to help us reach our goals.

Today's check-in was a little different than like what we did last week because Dr. Nick had us meet a life-size cardboard cut-out guy in his office. We were told his name was W.W. Dr. Nick said that W.W. doesn't really do anything other than just sit there.

We went through check-in talking about our past week with family, school, and friends. Sometimes, I noticed Dr. Nick would paste a little round sticker to W.W. whenever anyone in our group talked about stuff that was worrying or bothering them. Like, when this girl said her family might be moving pretty soon or when Thomas said his dad was getting re-married again, the counselor pasted a little round sticker to W.W.'s face. By the time we got done with check-in, W.W. had a face full of little round stickers! He looked like my cousin who has pimples all over his face.

We got to do the counseling activity as soon as check-in was over. Dr. Nick said he wanted us to come up with a list of things that kids like us might worry about. He used the whiteboard to keep track of what everybody said. The list started with just one or two things, but then everybody started having fun writing stuff on the board!

Homework, grades, being liked, making teams, and chores seemed to worry nearly everybody. Some kids worry about getting into trouble, not having enough money, not having friends, and not fitting in with the other kids at school. Some kids worry about moving, like that girl in our group. I was going to say something like how I worry about being alone at night, but I didn't want to sound like I was scared. When we were done, we had a huge list of worries!

I was really surprised when Dr. Nick gave us all a helium balloon and a marker! I love stuff like that! I really wanted the big green balloon, but I didn't get that one. I got the blue one instead. I don't think Dr. Nick liked that I kept asking him for the green balloon. He told me, "You don't always get what you want, but you do get to make the most of what you get." I had no idea what he said, but I could tell by the way he said it I wasn't going to get the green balloon. Oh well, blue is a good color, and it's better than nothing.

Dr. Nick told us to think of one of those things we worry about. It could be something at home, in school, or with friends. He even said we could use one of the worries from our list on the whiteboard or even a different one.

Once we figured out what our worry was, we were supposed to write it on our balloon with the marker he gave us. Like, on my balloon I wrote the words "Night time." When everybody wrote something, Dr. Nick helped us tie a string to our balloon. The other end of the string was connected to our chair.

Dr. Nick then told everybody to leave the balloons alone and to slide our chairs back against the wall and then to kneel around the table. He gave everybody a sheet of paper, and this time, asked us to come up with a don't worry plan. On our paper we were told to write like a three-step plan that would take the place of our worry. I was glad that he gave us an example of what he wanted us to do.

He used a word from this girl's balloon that read "failing" on it. So, on her paper the counselor helped her come up with a plan that had three or four things she could do to help her not worry abut failing. Dr. Nick called this her success plan. The plan said she should be coming to school on time with all her school stuff and a good attitude. The second thing on her plan was about her following school rules, doing homework, and reading every day for twenty to thirty minutes. I think the last thing on her list was to ask for help whenever she needed it.

We got to vote if the plan sounded like it would be a good one. Like if the girl just did the stuff written on the paper she would probably pass. We all voted that it was a pretty good plan. Now she wouldn't have anything left to worry about!

This whole thing about coming up with a success plan took a little while. Some of us, like mostly me, was getting bored. One kid tried to take my blue balloon, and I tried to remember what Dr. Nick told me. Even though I couldn't quite remember what he said, I tried to say it just like Dr. Nick told me. I said, "You've got one already so deal with it!" Once we all got our success plans done, Dr. Nick let us read our plans out loud.

When that was done, we got to go outside with our worry balloons in one hand and our success plans in our pockets or zipped inside our backpacks. We walked out to the field, and Dr. Nick said in an important voice that we didn't have to worry anymore about whatever the word on our balloon was because we have a success plan to take its place. He also said that knowing how to let go of worry is a great feeling and that sooner or later, all of our worries will disappear out of sight.

We began counting down from ten to one. On one, we let our worry balloons go. It was really awesome! It was a blast watching all those balloons fly away. We just stood there until we couldn't see them anymore! Dr. Nick told me he thought my blue balloon was really taking off fast.

Once we couldn't see our balloons anymore, Dr. Nick had us pull out our success plans and told us to show them to our teachers and parents.

Just about before we left, Dr. Nick asked us if anyone knew what the initials W.W. stood for. No one did but everybody guessed. One kid said it stood for Willy Wonka. That made pretty good sense because my grandma says that candy causes pimply skin. We followed Dr. Nick back into his office where he had us meet his friend, Worry Wart, who doesn't have a success plan, he just sits there and worries.

I got it.

Dear Parent,

Be sure to ask your child about the helium balloon he or she had been given. Thing is, your child was told to let it go! The idea behind today's counseling activity was to help your child learn how to "let go" of useless worries. In place of worry, students in counseling group developed a strategic plan to address whatever it was they were worried about. For example, instead of worrying about failing, one student came up with a plan when, where, and how often to study. No more worry! Guess what worried your child?

FORGIVENESS

Goal of Activity: To encourage the student to broaden his or her personal understanding of the term forgiveness. The student will also learn how to use forgiveness as a tool to promote personal growth.

Student Mix: boys and girls of approximately the same age and grade

Group Size: six to eight students

Suggested Time: thirty-five to forty-five minutes

Materials Required: pencils, erasers, paper, and forgiveness cards

Considerations:

Some girls and boys are reluctant to let go of their anger, bitterness, envy, and guilt. That's all they've ever had to hold on to. Learning how to forgive someone is really a pretty scary proposition. It means letting go, and letting go for most kids that often don't have anything to begin with, doesn't come easy. It certainly won't be accomplished because of one activity, but it can be the start of learning.

Remember, forgiveness is a process. Seldom (if ever) do boys and girls just suddenly wake up and say, "I'm prepared and willing to forgive all the people in my life who have done me wrong." Willingness to forgive is a good start. Learning how to forgive and being able to maintain forgiveness over a period of time is something we can help the student with.

Teaching a student how to forgive is certainly different than teaching them to forgive. Be sure you clarify this point with your students and their parents. Helping a student learn how to forgive is a lot like many other skills we hope to equip students with. If and whenever the time comes for the student to offer forgiveness, he or she will be able to.

Student Reflection:

I was really in a bad mood today. I was so mad at this one kid for what he was saying about me to the whole school during recess! I was just about to beat him up when the freeze bell rang. My teacher talked to me, and she had me sitting by myself in our room after we got back to class. She was also calling my counselor, and I could hear her ask if she could send me over to his office.

I got to his office with a note my teacher had written. Dr. Nick seemed really glad to see me again. He had a place for me with this different group of kids. We did check-in and talked about stuff that was going on over the past week with family, school, and friends. Dr. Nick told us that how good we do in the future might have a lot to do with how well we're doing right now with family, school, and friends. He said that no matter how hard or frustrating stuff in our life gets, that it's important we hang in there and ask for help whenever we need it.

I wasn't much in the mood to be talking. I just sat there with my arms across my chest. I was still feeling pretty mad, and I could tell my face was feeling really hot. Pretty soon though, I also started feeling like I didn't want these different kids seeing me this way.

After we were done doing check-in, Dr. Nick gave everybody

a sheet of paper and a pencil to write with. The counselor asked each one of us if we'd write down the name of one or two people that we felt did a wrong thing against us. Like, he said to think of someone we know that maybe was an ex-friend who stole our bike, a neighbor who broke our window, or even someone in our family who did something to make us not trust them anymore.

Chaw! The only name I wrote across my paper in really big fat letters was Omar. He was the kid I was going to beat up! I also put down like two other names, but I wrote them really small. The girl next to me, Susan, wrote the name of her Uncle Bob on her paper. I looked at another kid's paper, and I heard Dr. Nick remind everyone they needed to MYOB and keep their eyes on their own papers. I kept my paper covered after I heard him say that!

Once everybody had written some names, Dr. Nick told us to raise our hands. He then called on volunteers to read the names from their lists out loud. He also made everyone tell why the names were written on the list.

Even though he said we didn't have to read our names out loud and tell about why if we didn't want to, he told everybody about keeping the stuff we talk about here in our group private. Like he said, "Nobody blabbers this stuff to anybody else that's not in our group or else."

Susan said the reason her uncle is not her favorite uncle anymore because he stays at her home all day and eats all their food. She also said that her dad was going to kick his butt the next time he trashes the house with all his free-loading, drug-smoking, and worthless friends.

One of the other names on my list was my babysitter. Dr. Nick asked me if I wanted to tell why the babysitter made my list. I was still feeling pretty mad about stupid Omar when he told me to tell him why about the babysitter. I told him because she made my mom unhappy. Before I knew it, I told Dr. Nick and everyone else about what happened. Some days my dad would come home sooner than he mostly does. He and the babysitter would go into my dad's room and sort laundry. My mom came home one time when they were in there, and my mom got really mad and was sad and was yelling like all at the same time. The cops then came a little bit later on and took her to the hospital for being so mad and sad.

My counselor told me he would like to talk to me later by myself about what I had said if it would be okay with me. I said all right, but I sure felt embarrassed and a little guilty even though I don't know why. I just wanted to be quiet for awhile.

After all the kids who wanted to say something about the names on their lists talked, Dr. Nick told everybody to lean to the left and scribble lightly across that other person's paper. I couldn't believe he just gave the kid sitting next to me permission to scribble on my paper! I was mad again!

Dr. Nick then went to the whiteboard and wrote the word forgiveness. He asked us what the word meant. We had like five kids in our group and everyone said something. We got the list down to mean a couple things. This is what we got: Not being mad and/or sad anymore with a person who did something we didn't like and giving that person an ongoing second chance, but maybe not forgetting what that person did to get us mad or hurt our feelings in the first place.

Dr. Nick said it would be really important that we ask our parents and grandparents for their definition of the word forgiveness too. He says that it's always good to know what the important grown-ups in our lives think about stuff like that.

Our counselor said, in some ways, forgiveness might be like erasing a pencil mark someone had made on our paper. Like, even if the person who scribbled on our paper feels guilty or sad about what they've done, it still takes a lot of effort to erase what someone else has messed up.

Dr. Nick told us the first step in forgiveness starts with giving ourselves permission to get over it. Getting over it means not being angry or having a bitter feeling toward that person anymore. He says the next thing in forgiving somebody means to concentrate on what we're doing for ourselves, rather than what someone else did or didn't do. Dr. Nick said if it helps, we can think of forgiveness like this. Pretend anger, betrayal, disappointment, and other feelings we get that we have toward somebody is like an icy cold, barren place. Learning how to climb up and out of that place is a lot like the effort it takes to forgive somebody. If you're not careful and determined to get out, it's easy to fall right back down to where you started.

That made pretty good sense. So, like with Susan whose uncle is causing such a stink at their house, we talked about how she should just concentrate on the stuff she can take care of. I told her she should hide the remote and put a lock on the refrigerator. She should even find her uncle a newspaper so he can look for a job.

Dr. Nick said he understands why Susan probably doesn't look up to her uncle like she used to and that she's very disappointed in his behavior. I just think he sounds like a loser, but I don't want to hurt Susan's feelings. Instead of telling her that, I just wrote it down in really tiny letters next to the last name on my paper.

When Dr. Nick looked at me and asked how I was feeling and if I wanted to hear something he had been thinking about the babysitter story, I shrugged my shoulders and said, "Sure." Dr. Nick said he thought I was very brave and he was proud of me for telling him about how things are going on at home. He told me that he doesn't know if I'm disappointed in the babysitter, my dad, my mom, or just with everything.

What he said next really caught me by surprise. He said, "Most of all, the one person you shouldn't be disappointed in or angry with is yourself. You have nothing to feel ashamed of or guilty about and it wasn't your fault." He also asked me to think about if any of what was going on at home had anything to do with what Omar was talking about. I think I was feeling embarrassed, but I was smiling too. I'm not sure why, but I think I felt better because someone else knows and I didn't have to say anything.

When we left counseling group today, Dr. Nick gave everybody a forgiveness card that had an eraser taped to it. On the back of the card it read: "Forgiveness gives the forgiven a brand new start and can erase all the forgiver's leftover, sad, and angry feelings."

Dr. Nick kept me back for a few minutes after the other kids left. He asked me how my mom was doing and where my dad is staying at. I told him my mom is out of the hospital but still cries a lot. He told me he understands why I'm so mad all the time and why I get upset so fast. He also asked me to talk with my mom about our activity today and find out what forgiveness means to her. Dr. Nick said she might be sort of feeling like I do.

Dear Parent,

Today's counseling activity dealt with the concept of "Forgiveness." What it is, what it's suppose to do, and how to give it were questions that everyone was encouraged to discuss with their families and find answers to. During group, your child had the opportunity to think about those questions. The person sitting next to them had scribbled on their paper. We compared the similarities of "erasing" unwanted marks with that of forgiving someone of unwanted deeds. Be sure to ask your child about his or her responses.

RECOGNIZING FRIENDS

Goal of Activity: To help the student develop a broader perspective in the understanding of how their friendships are subject to change over time.

Student Mix: boys and girls of similar age and grade

Group Size: four to six students

Suggested Time: twenty to thirty minutes

Materials Required: four large grocery bags, paper, and lollipops

Considerations:

This is a really neat activity to help students understand how the dynamics of friendships can operate. For many boys and girls, especially those students who are in counseling, the making and maintaining of friendships is a mysterious process that seems to rely on the giving and receiving of gifts and favors. It's heart breaking to see kids give their favorite things away in hopes of receiving friendship in return.

Students are often easily frustrated when their like of someone doesn't automatically translate into a great and wonderful friendship with the person of their choice. Often, this frustration leads to further failure in their quest to make and maintain friendships.

The activity also addresses how friendships can change over time. In school, students know better than most people that last year's best friend can easily turn into this year's worst enemy. Learning how to understand and deal with the concept that best friends make the worst enemies is something that all boys and girls should learn.

As counselors, we have a unique opportunity to provide students with the tools to become successful in not only making and maintaining friendships, but to also broaden their understanding of what a friend actually is and can become.

Student Reflection:

I was late to school this morning. I hate being late, everybody looks at me weird when I go into my classroom. The part I hate most is when I go to the office to get my late slip and Sue, the office boss lady, says, "Well, why are you late this time?"

My counselor, Dr. Nick had already called my classroom looking for me. My teacher told him I was absent. She sent me over to his office, and I walked in and sat down in my usual spot. Three other kids were already there, and I was glad that this one girl I like was sitting there by where I usually sit. Dr. Nick told me he was very glad to see me and that I'm welcome any time I can make it.

I think I must have missed most of goal review and part of check-in. Even though I came late to group, I noticed Dr. Nick was asking lots of questions about our friends. His weirdest question was, "Why do you like your friends?" I thought it was funny to hear so many of the kids in our group use the word friend to explain why he or she likes the friend they were trying to describe!

When Dr. Nick asked me to explain why I like my friends, I said, "Because we always hang out with each other and do what each other wants to do no matter what." Since I was the last one in group to be asked that question, we started our counseling activity right after I finished my answer.

Our counselor taped three big brown grocery store paper sacks to the wall. Each bag had a word or two written on them. The words were friend, good friend, and best friend. He then asked us to come up with definitions for each type of friend, and he used the whiteboard to write our answers just above each paper sack.

This took a little while to do, and I think it was more Dr. Nick's answers than ours but that was all right. Even though this part of the activity took forever, this is what we came up with:

Friend: A friend is someone we like, know, and trust pretty well. Friends are also willing not to care about the little, goofy things that their friends do like saying "um" all the time.

Good Friend: A good friend is someone we like a lot, know, and trust even more than a friend. A good friend is usually willing to forgive their good friend for messing up sort of important things like not keeping every secret they're told.

Best Friend: A best friend is someone we like a whole bunch and is someone we know and trust even more than a good friend. Best friends will forgive their best friend lots of times, even for doing dumb things or messing up really important things, like talking about who we like to someone else.

Dr. Nick gave everyone three little half sheets of paper and told us to write the name of a friend on one sheet of paper, the name of a good friend on the second sheet of paper, and the name of one of our best friends on the third piece of paper.

I sat for just a second and thought of all my friends. I have lots of friends! Who would I choose? Jenna kept looking over at my paper to see if I'd written her name yet. She's not only my friend, but she's also my girlfriend! Once I was finished, Dr. Nick said to place our names in the matching sacks taped to the wall.

Our counselor then stuck a fourth sack to the wall, this sack had the word enemy written on it. I nearly blurted out the names of the kids I don't like, but just as I was going to say their names, Dr. Nick looked at me and said, "Don't even think about it!" How did he know I was going to yell those names out?

With Dr. Nick's help, we came up with a pretty good definition for the word enemy.

Enemy: A person that is very much disliked or even hated. A person who also very much dislikes or hates the person that hates them. An enemy is also someone who tries to make life hard for the person they don't like.

Talking about enemies really got some kids pretty fired up. Everybody had somebody they wanted to fight and punch. We were told to calm down and save our energy for making things better, not even, or even worse.

The counselor went to the wall and pulled a name out of the best friend sack and placed that name in the enemy sack. He said something about if anyone has ever had a best friend turn into an enemy. Lots of hands went up. He then asked us this next question: "How many of you know someone who lets a person go back and forth between being a best friend and an enemy?"

Oh baby! You should have heard all the kids talk! It sounded like a TV talk show! Lots of us talked about kids who are a best friend one day and like a day later, an enemy.

Sometimes it's over dumb things like stupid stuff. Dr. Nick says it might have something to do with learning how to build boundaries and set limits (whatever that meant), but also said he would talk about that another day.

Our counselor then spent the next few minutes moving names from one sack to another and asking the same type of questions. Questions like, "Have you ever had an enemy become a friend? Have you ever had a friend turn into a good friend? Have you ever had a best friend turn back into just a friend?"

We then talked about how confusing and frustrating it can be to like someone but not know how to turn that like into a good friendship. Dr. Nick said, "No matter how much we like someone or want to be liked by someone, good friendships take more than just liking each other." I thought about that, but I mostly thought that I like Jenna a whole lot because she's really pretty, plus she likes to borrow stuff from just me.

Our counselor gave me and everybody else a card with these words written on it: "If you have a friend who would lie for you, then you probably have a friend who would lie to you." We talked only for a minute or two about what that could mean. I thought maybe it had something to do with my friend lying to me about not getting into trouble if we hung out in the park before school, even though I'd be late. Dr. Nick said to take the card home and ask family members and friends what they think the card means.

As we left group, Dr. Nick gave everyone a treat and told us that we should always choose our friends wisely. If we're not sure if someone is a friend, think about the card he gave us today. While we were on our way back to the classroom, Jenna told me she would put my name on the top of her boyfriend list if I would borrow her some money for lunch! You bet I did! She's awesome and pretty, plus she even likes me more now!!!

Dear Parent,

In counseling group today your child participated in an activity that helps boys and girls figure out how their friendships work. We began with trying to understand the differences between friends, good friends, best friends, and enemies. We also examined how friends can slide back and forth along that continuum. The goal in today's activity was intended to help your child realize that friendships aren't just about liking someone. Trust, shared history, and common values all matter too.

THE GREAT MASQUERADE

Goal of Activity: To help increase the student's awareness of how deception works, how to avoid be being deceived, and what to do in the event a significant deception occurs.

Student Mix: boys and girls of similar age and grade

Group Size: four to six students

Suggested Time: thirty-five to forty-five minutes

Materials Required: three cans of vegetables with laminated labels, index cards, and treats

Considerations:

Some of the boys and girls we see in counseling will have been exposed to inappropriate adult and peer-related behaviors. A few of the kids we see will be already identified as having been exposed, most will not. This activity helps teach a valuable lesson for all students to learn regarding deception and how to deal with it appropriately.

Embarrassment, anger, and guilt are often attributed to the obstacles kids face in reporting being victims of inappropriate conduct. Being tricked into such conduct for many boys and girls often implies a sense of participation on some level.

In many areas of a student's life, participation often translates into mutual consent. For example, two kids who get into a fight at school. Even though one kid may have started the fight, the other student is frequently persuaded by the principal to believe that he or she may have actually chosen to participate in the fight based on the student's response. Later, as the student tries to understand his or her involvement in the incident, the student may come to the realization that he or she may have had several choices at the time of the fight. One option was to have walked away; another option was to yell to the yard duty that a problem was happening. In the absence of being able to fully understand the complexities and limitations of his or her emotional abilities at that time, the student may then conclude that he or she did, in fact, willingly participate in the event.

If you choose to present this activity to your group, as with the lesson "Keeping Secrets," be mindful that jiggling at locked doors may prove to be somewhat of a perilous endeavor. Remember, you may be tugging on doors some girls and boys prefer to keep locked. Consider that some stories may be better left untold, at least until another time. Determining which doors to unlock should be based on, in part, the degree to which the student's behavior is dysfunctional and counterproductive.

Student Reflection:

Our school counselor, Dr. Nick, called for me just before break. This is the first time I've ever had to choose between break and counseling. I like both, and picking one over the other was pretty hard. Today I chose to go to counseling because counseling only happens once a week. Besides, it was raining outside, and I was hungry.

Sometimes, like today, new kids show up when other boys and girls stop coming. Dr. Nick says he understands that kids may need to take a break from counseling. He explained that, first of all, kids really learn a lot about themselves, their families, and their friends in counseling, and sometimes it takes time to figure out what it all means. He says that taking time off from counseling also gives us the chance to practice some of the stuff we've learned in group, like working better and smarter toward reaching our goals.

On the whiteboard, Dr. Nick had drawn two lines that went from one side of the board to the other. The lines divided the whiteboard into three parts. We took turns writing the names of our most important family members on the bottom part of the whiteboard. Our teachers' and friends' names were written in the middle of the board. We left the very top of the whiteboard blank.

For check-in our counselor pointed to the family members' names that were written on the whiteboard and asked, "Who can tell me all about this person?" The one name he pointed to was my older stepbrother. I told Dr. Nick all about him. I even told Dr. Nick about Tuesday night. That's the night the police came to our house and took him to jail for kicking his girlfriend who's going to have a baby.

Dr. Nick pointed out lots more names, and each time someone in our group told about that person. He did the same thing for the teacher and the friends group of names. I liked doing check-in this way!

Our counselor can't really draw very well, but he still tries anyway. On the whiteboard, he drew a picture of tree. He said to imagine that each one of us is sort of like a tree. Our family is our roots, and our school and friends are like our trunk. At the very top of the tree we hold up our arms above our heads and reach as high as we hope to go in the future! He had us all stand and reach as high up as we could!

Dr. Nick asked all of us what we want to be when we get older. He wrote our answers at the very top of the whiteboard, where the tree branches were. I said I wanted to become a policeman. Clint said he's going to drop out of college and be a professional football player. This other girl told us she just wants to get her own trailer but to keep it on its wheels so she could travel and maybe go to college.

I never thought of me being like a tree and my family being like my roots. That was kind of neat!

After check-in, Dr. Nick put three cans of vegetables on the table. One can was corn, another was a can of peas, and the third can was a can of beans. He told us to point to the can of corn if we knew which one it was. Duh.

Next, he took the labels off the cans and switched them all around. Dr. Nick said to watch carefully as he exchanged labels. He asked us to point to the can of corn again. Even though we had some arguing, I was really pretty sure I wasn't tricked. I pointed to the can that I thought had corn in it. Not having anyone else point to the can I was pointing to made me feel a little less sure though.

Dr. Nick took all the labels off again and mixed the bare cans around. He then put the labels back on the cans. Again he asked, "Which can has the corn in it?"

By now no one knew the answer to that question and what happened next was the biggest surprise of all! Dr. Nick put the three cans in front of us, took off all their labels, and told us the truth, none of the cans had corn in them! On top of that, he said none of them were even vegetables and that all three cans have fruit cocktail in them! He tricked us, and you know what? I don't like being tricked. Ever!

Our counselor promised us that he didn't really actually trick us. Yeah, right. He said to think about this, "What if, we tricked ourselves into believing that things are exactly the way they always look." I didn't get it. He told me to think about Halloween when people disguise themselves with costumes and masks. That I got.

Kinda like the cans, Dr. Nick says that some people on purpose wear false costumes to fool others. Our counselor said that sometimes the people we would be most surprised by wear some of the most trickiest disguises.

Using that Halloween example, the counselor asked, "Who is the most kindest and nicest kid you know?" I told him the name of the boy who sits behind me in class, "Bobby." Dr. Nick said, "Good. Now imagine Bobby wearing a ferocious, evil, and scary costume. If you didn't know it was Bobby and you didn't know it was a costume, you might think that person might really be ferocious, evil, and scary."

He told us to remember the can of corn activity. He said, "Remember, things aren't always like they look."

As far as costumes and disguises go, our counselor said that costumes and disguises don't need to be made up. There are lots of people who wear disguises of everyday people. Some of those disguises or costumes might be like:

The too helpful stranger.

The good neighbor who asks me to keep bad secrets.

The family member who will blame me for ruining the family.

The coach or teacher who has off task private sessions with me.

A church person who wants to do more than church work.

The friend who wants what's best for only him/herself.

Our group talked about how confusing and hard it can be to see through these disguises, especially when bad people wear really good disguises. Like for example, the people we hear about on TV and radio doing bad things to trick or fool good people.

One girl in our group said she told a teacher at her old school about the time her cousin played a card game with her. The cousin told this girl, "You're supposed to take off some clothes if you're given a card with black or red on it." Dr. Nick told her she did the right thing by telling her teacher because tricks like that have to be reported right now, just like when we talked about in that MYOB activity we did that one time.

Dr. Nick says we have to be careful because anyone can be a master of disguise, even someone we already know. The counselor told us that the master of disguise is someone who is very tricky and tries to take advantage of certain people who make good targets.

Dr. Nick then said what he meant by the words good target and wrote this on the whiteboard:

A Target is . . .

✿A person who can be any age, young or old.

✿A person who wants to be liked no matter what.

✿A person who will not question what someone else tells them to do.

✿A person who will feel responsible for anything wrong that happens.

✿A person who has a hard time talking about themselves.

I heard him say those things, and I was thinking that some of those things sound a little bit like me.

Dr. Nick said anyone could be tricked or fooled by anyone at any time and anywhere! Snap! Talking about all this stuff was creeping me out! I wanted to change the subject because I was feeling really nervous. I didn't want Dr. Nick to ask me if I've ever been tricked. I don't think I would have answered his question because I don't want to talk about some things that only my last counselor knows about.

Dr. Nick said we should have two goals. The first goal is not to be tricked. The second goal should be what to do when we are tricked. The counselor asked all of us to come up with a list of ten people that we would tell if we were fooled by a master of disguise. He also wanted us to think about what if one of the ten people on our list turned out to be the person that tricked us. What would we do then?

We got to keep our list, and the counselor gave everyone a treat for coming to counseling group. He told us we could have a sucker but not to be one. He said that meant even if we ever get tricked or fooled, the worst part is not telling somebody about it.

While we were leaving group he told us, "If I ever do anything wrong that hurts or bothers you, I want you to tell your teacher, your principal, and your parents." He really looked serious, and I believed him. I wish my other counselor would have said that.

Dear Parent,

The goal of today's activity was intended to broaden your child's awareness of "things aren't always as they appear to be." Being young and naïve are variables that certain people look to take advantage of. In a non-threatening way, the boys and girls in group were introduced to this concept through the means of identifying a can of corn amidst several cans of vegetables. However, unbeknown to them, the can had a corn label over its original fruit cocktail label. Talk about assuming the truth!

THE BRIDGE

Goal of Activity: To expand the student's awareness of how the concept of time must be factored into the development of career and occupational goals. Students will also develop a greater understanding for the importance of recognizing, selecting, and maintaining supports throughout their lives.

Student Mix: boys and girls of similar age and grade

Group Size: six to twelve students

Suggested Time: thirty to forty minutes

Materials Required: picture of a bridge, pencil, paper, and a roll of toilet paper

Considerations:

This is a lesson that can help boys and girls establish a better sense of how the concept of time needs to be factored into development of their goals. This also makes for a great classroom introduction into counseling activity. Students generally have a good time in this activity and will make the connection between getting from point A to point B. When you turn point A into where they are now in life and designate point B as the place they want to be one day, that's the moment they begin to understand what the activity is all about.

Many of these students know all too well about supports coming and going in their lives. A lot of kids have too few supports through death, divorce, abandonment, betrayal, or incarceration. Some kids will have too many supports such as parents, stepparents, grandparents, and aunts or uncles who push and shove one another to become the student's most significant support. Children will, however, experience having someone in their lives let them down. When that inevitably happens, it becomes our primary objective as counselors conducting this lesson to help kids understand that everyone has the responsibility of not only building their own bridge, but to get to the other side, regardless of how many supports are in place and how long it may take.

Student Reflection:

This morning as I was sitting at my desk, my teacher told me to go to the office to see a guy named Dr. Nick. I guess he's the school counselor. I'm new to this school, and I haven't met too many people yet. I wasn't sure why I had to go see the counselor anyway.

I found his office and went in. There was a pretty big group of kids in there sitting around a table. I'd figured there must have been six or seven kids in his office, not counting me. Dr. Nick introduced himself and said he heard I was new. He asked me to join his counseling group for the day along with some other kids. I said, "Yeah, whatever."

He thought we should get started by introducing ourselves. We took turns saying our name, grade, age, and where we're from. The counselor also had us say what we want to have as a future occupation, like a job or something.

Even though I'm new here, these kids seemed not so much different than the ones at my old school. Nearly everyone in this group said something about becoming a professional athlete, a rock star, or a movie star. I didn't want to become any of those things, and I told them so. I said, "The only thing I want to be when I get older is to be rich!" I felt pretty smart when everyone laughed.

After we did that junk, we did this thing called check-in. The other kids seemed to know all about it. The counselor wanted us to say something about our families, school, and friends. It seemed pretty stupid and I didn't say much of anything, but I did figure I could impress them if I said something that would get their attention. Besides, there was this one pretty good looking girl in the room, and I'm pretty sure she liked me already.

When it was my turn to talk about my family, I just told them it was just me and my mom at home. I also told them that my older brother was in this job core program someplace and that we had just moved here to get away from the gangs in our old neighborhood. Not all of that was quite true, but I thought it sounded pretty good.

Dr. Nick showed us some pictures, and one of those pictures was of the Golden Gate Bridge in San Francisco. I told everybody I'd been on that bridge lots of times. He then asked us some questions about bridges. We were asked to name three famous bridges, name materials bridges are made of, and for us to explain why bridges are even made in the first place.

The counselor gave everyone a half sheet of paper and told us to:

List up to five names of people we depend on.

List the name of our best friends from a long time ago and the name of our best friend today.

List the names of any of our family members who have either gone away or have passed away.

Write the name of a person who's really let us down.

If you could build a bridge from your front door to anywhere in the world you wanted, where would it be?

Personally, I don't like to get into all of that imaginary fantasy stuff, but I noticed most the other kids in group were taking what this guy said pretty seriously. I just scribbled a couple names on the piece of paper and was going to mumble my way through any questions the counselor might ask me later.

I did feel a little bit excited though when the counselor said we were actually going to build a bridge! Then he said we weren't going to use the regular building materials like steel, iron, and concrete. He told us that our bridge would be made of toilet paper! I said, "That sounds like a crappy idea!" The other kids laughed and the counselor even laughed a little bit too.

Dr. Nick said since everyone was very familiar and experienced with the building material, two people were picked to hold the ends of like a twenty-foot strip of toilet paper that was stretched across the room. He then took volunteers to act as supports for the bridge. I was one of those support people who was told to stand alongside the bridge and place my open hands very lightly under the paper trail.

The counselor had people coming and going all the time, but the two end people always stayed the same. Sometimes there would only be one or two people supporting the bridge. Sometimes four or five people would have to squeeze together to support it. There was one or two times when no one was supporting the bridge at all. How that all happened was that the counselor would have the two people at either ends of the bridge take turns answering his questions. Like I remember him asking things like:

Choose two people in this room to be supports that have your best interests in mind.

Sit down one support person most likely to eventually let you down.

Choose two people to be supports that may still be your friend ten years from now.

Sit down a support person most likely to drop out of high school.

Call on a person you don't know very well for support.

Sit down a person who you think is really good at causing chaos.

Choose a support person most inclined to keep his or her priorities of faith, family, and friends first.

Sit down the least responsible person supporting the bridge.

Call on someone for support who you think might be rich one day.

Sit down someone you would have a hard time saying "no" to.

This whole thing of coming and going had gone on for a really long time. Just as I started to wipe my nose on the bridge, the counselor had us go back to our table. He wanted to talk about the answers we had written on our papers before we began building the bridge.

Dr. Nick said that bridges connect two points and allow passage from one point to another. He said those points not only connect, like two cities, but they may also connect where you are now to where you hope to be in the future.

He then asked me how long it usually takes me to go from one end of the Golden Gate Bridge to the other. Well, I really didn't know. I had actually lied when I told everyone I had been on it lots of times. "Twenty to forty minutes," I told him. I was pretty relieved when he agreed that it might take that long to cross the Golden Gate Bridge.

He told me to think about where I am right now and imagine where I want to be in the future. He said it won't take just a few minutes to get there, it will take years. Whoa! The counselor said that it's important to set goals, like where we want to get to in our life. He then reminded us of what we all had said about what we wanted to become one day.

Dr. Nick looked at me and said, "I want you to be rich one day too, but you're not rich right now and you need to figure out how you're going to go from not rich to rich because it's going to take a lot longer than twenty to forty minutes."

He told us, but I felt like he was looking right at me, that it's important to recognize the supports we have in place right now, even if they're not exactly the ones we want. He said it's going to be important to learn how to not only ask for helpers but be able to sit down or remove the ones that aren't really helping at all. He also said that sometimes it's hard getting used to supports like a grandma or grandpa who aren't around anymore. Man, I really think he was talking about me, and I didn't like it!

The counselor backed off a little bit and said we all need to look at family, teachers, and friends as well as other things like food, clothing, and housing that we depend on. He also said that the most famous and important bridge in the world is going to be the one we build for ourselves.

He caught me off guard again when he told me that if I don't get a destination of where I want to be and how I'm going to get there figured out pretty soon, one day will come and it's going to be too late to build a very worthwhile bridge. I felt like he was trying to scare me like everyone else tries to do. He didn't sound angry, but he did sound as if it were important that I hear what he said. How he said that stuff made me feel I had to hurry up and do something!

The other kids got to read their answers to the questions he had asked about family, friends, the jerks that betrayed us, and people like my grandma, who isn't around anymore. I still just pretty much sat and listened to what the other kids said. I really didn't have any answers of my own that I had written down or wanted to think about. Dr. Nick told me that was another example of me not actively participating in my own life. What did he mean by that? I was really getting pissed off at him for embarrassing me in front of everyone else! I got up and left group and went back to my classroom.

Later that day I was having lunch with some kids, and the girl that liked me from group came over and asked to talk to me! I knew she liked me. She said I was wrong for walking out of counseling group this morning. The counselor was just trying to help me understand that I've got to do something with my life.

My new babe told me that the counselor helped her understand that if she doesn't get her own life together, no matter how many supports she has, that she'll end up going nowhere in her life too. She said, "Dr. Nick told me people will come and go in my life, and there will be times I feel like I'm all alone. No matter what happens though, to remember not to forget the main reason I began building my bridge in the first place."

The girl told me she hoped I heard what she said. She also told me I was a jerk. I don't think she meant it though because most of my girlfriends start out liking me this way. She'll come around.

Dr. Nick called me to his office just before school got out for

the day. He asked me to sit down, but I told him, "I don't have to."
He apologized for not making my first time in counseling more
enjoyable. I didn't say anything or really look at him very much.
I think I was still feeling mad and even a little embarrassed, but
mostly mad.

He said he knew a little bit about me before I came to group
this morning because he had looked through my school records.
I told him I had heard some things about him too. He invited
me to attend counseling group next week, and I told him, "Yeah,
maybe, whatever," and then I left his office.

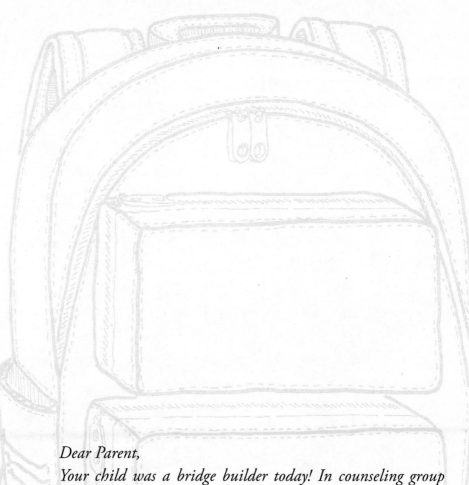

Dear Parent,

Your child was a bridge builder today! In counseling group students participated in an activity that helped them understand how important it is to build a connection to their future. In using the "building bridge" analogy, the lesson encouraged kids to start figuring out where they want to go in life. More specifically, what type of career to pursue. The bridge may take years to complete and plenty of supports will come and go along the way, but no matter what, build that bridge!

I'VE GOT A SECRET

Goal of Activity: To help the student learn to question him/herself in determining the appropriateness of keeping certain secrets.

Student Mix: boys and girls of approximately the same age and grade

Group Size: four to six students

Suggested Time: twenty-five to thirty-five minutes

Materials Required: one paper sack, two to three dozen paper strips, copies of activity questions, and treats

Considerations:

Students are frequently asked to keep secrets. Most secrets probably involve insignificant things. Some secrets, however, are very significant and have the potential to shape a young person's life in ways he or she can't begin to understand at this early age.

Helping a student learn to differentiate between good and bad secrets will be an ongoing process for everyone involved. For boys and girls, the process of interpreting and deciphering relevant information is at the core of their decision-making abilities.

This activity will be a useful tool in helping your students learn to develop their decision-making skills. When boys and girls learn how to question themselves about the secrets they keep, they are ultimately making decisions about the types of emotional baggage they will carry with them throughout their lives.

Student Reflection:

I was pretty careful that the yard duty lady didn't see me run to counseling this morning. If I can be the first person in counseling group, I usually get to choose the best chair to sit in before everybody else does.

When I got there, I was disappointed that Dr. Nick had taken the soft chair from his office. The only good chair left was the counselor's chair, and I asked him as nicely as I could, "May I please sit in your chair today?"

Dr. Nick looked at me kind of funny, leaned over, and asked me if I could keep a secret. I said, "You bet!" Then he said, "Perfect, because that's exactly what we'll be keeping in our activity today." I didn't quite understand his answer, but I was feeling pretty excited.

Our group had just two of us girls and three boys. I nearly died when my brother showed up for our group! He's such a blabber mouth! I won't be able to say anything with him here. He made it four boys to only two girls!

We started counseling group with introductions and check-in. My brother kept interrupting me when it was my turn to talk about family! I wanted to kill him and just about did! Dr. Nick told me he understands that I'm feeling frustrated and mad. He also said that I'm acting like how maybe some grown-ups might act too about my brother's teasing but to still do my very best.

I was glad that the counselor kept telling my brother to be polite, patient, and thoughtful while other people were talking. I would've been gladder if he told him just to shut up. I was really glad when he also told my brother he wasn't earning his treat for the day.

After I finished saying my part about family, school, and friends, it was my brother's turn to talk. I couldn't believe he told everyone about my wetting the bed! I felt so mad and embarrassed that I began to cry and crawled under the table.

I've never heard Dr. Nick use the voice I heard him use! In a loud voice he said, "Time out!" Next thing I know, he's asking me if I'm all right and invited me to come out from under the table. I sat at the table but kept my head down. Dr. Nick told everyone else to put their heads down too.

I heard the counselor tell everybody that's it's important to respect each other's privacy. He said everyone has the right to keep parts of their life private unless that person gives someone else permission to talk about those things. Dr. Nick told us, "If you hear something about somebody from someone else, it's a rumor and don't believe it." I sure hoped he was giving my brother the evil eye while he was saying that!

After a couple minutes of keeping our heads down and being quiet, we got started with the counseling activity. Dr. Nick told us that our activity was going to be about keeping secrets. He showed us a sack filled with strips of paper, and each piece of paper had a secret written on it. He told us that every secret starts out with something, such as a family member, a stranger, or a good friend. Like, one thing read, "A family member gives you the secret of not telling your parents about the grape juice they spilled on the white rug."

We got to take turns taking a secret from the sack. We were told not to let anyone in the group know our secret. Once we all picked a secret, Dr. Nick chose one of us to be first to start the game.

The person he chose to go first was the other girl in our

group. She was told to stand up in front of everybody. The rest of us then could ask this girl any questions we wanted to about her secret. Dr. Nick told us we could use any of the questions he had already written on the whiteboard or make up one on our own. The big rule was that no one could ask the person with the secret what the secret was. We couldn't even guess at what he secret might be! The only thing we could do was to ask questions. Some of the types of questions the counselor wanted us to ask were things like:

Is your secret good or bad?

Might someone get hurt if you don't tell?

Is there a chance you'll get in trouble by telling?

What could happen if you told your secret?

Does your secret have anything to do with the law?

Do you want to be responsible for this secret?

If you decide to reveal the secret, name three people you might tell.

Would someone be upset with you if you shared the secret?

Would telling the secret mean you've broken a promise?

Is embarrassment, guilt, or shame keeping your secret safe?

Have you ever been in a situation like this before?

The way Dr. Nick sounded as he talked about secrets reminded me of the way he talked to me at the beginning of group when I asked if I could sit in his chair. He sounded really mysterious!

I was having a blast just asking questions because I wanted to sound mysterious too! Once we all had the chance to ask a question and then be asked questions about the secret we had, Dr. Nick called us all back to the table to talk about stuff. Our counselor said he wanted to tell us the secret about secrets.

Dr. Nick said that probably most everybody has secrets, and secrets are kept for different reasons. The biggest mystery he said about secrets is not so much figuring out what they are as much as why people keep them safe! He went to the whiteboard and wrote this: "Big secrets take a lot of energy and effort to keep safe."

I'm not really sure what he meant by keeping secrets safe, but I didn't want to ask either. I was glad when he explained what he meant by telling a story about two people. He talked about two people that have the same type of secret. One person tries really hard to keep the secret safe. Like, she may try not to think about the secret and even lie to family and friends for a really long time about the secret. Later, she might even try to forget the secret by using drugs and alcohol, but the harder she tries to keep her secret safe, the more energy she uses and the worse she feels.

The other person with the same secret chooses to handle her secret in a different way. She decides to tell only one or two other people she trusts about the secret she has. Her secret is still pretty private, but she shares it at the right time, in the right place, with the right person. This girl does not try to forget the secret and actually uses the secret as something to learn from rather than forget. The secret becomes less powerful, and the girl feels better because she hasn't tried so hard to keep it safe because she doesn't have to anymore. It sounded pretty confusing, but I sort of got it...sorta.

Dr. Nick said that maybe there's lots of people who share

different or the same types of secrets for the same reasons. Those reasons might be like to not feel embarrassment, shame, guilt, fear, or because of a promise made. He told us to think about the example of the two girls he had just given.

I was feeling as if everyone in our group kind of understood what he meant too. Even though he didn't ask anyone to tell any of their secrets, he did ask us to use our list of questions to help figure out why or if we should be keeping them. I felt better about myself as I sort of imagined that my secret didn't have to be such a big secret.

When the bell rang, Dr. Nick said he would be back next week, but he was also going to make some new group rules and stuff about who can be in groups. I'm pretty sure he gave me a wink when he said that.

He gave everyone a treat and a copy of the list of questions we used to ask each other during our activity. As I was running out of his office, I heard Dr. Nick yell out to us something about practice asking ourselves questions about which secrets we'll choose to keep safe.

Dear Parent,

In counseling group today, your child participated in an activity that dealt with the topic of "keeping secrets." Boys and girls, like many adults, keep secrets for a wide variety of reasons. However, shame, embarrassment, and guilt are often powerful motivators that serve to keep "bad" secrets safe. Children were encouraged to think about all the "whys" behind the secrets they may be keeping safe. More importantly, students were encouraged to seek counsel with trusted adults in times of uncertainty.

RIGHT, WRONG,
OR DEPENDS?

Goal of Activity: To help students not only develop a broader sense of right and wrong, but to also identify situation specific variables that may also factor into their decision-making process.

Student Mix: boys and girls of similar age and grade

Group Size: four to six students

Suggested Time: thirty to forty minutes

Materials Required: pencils, paper, parent question cards, and "Right makes Might" awards

Considerations:

This is a wonderful activity because it generates a lot of discussion surrounding what a young person thinks in terms of right and wrong. I also like this activity because we're helping kids learn to expand both the width and depth in their growing understanding of these concepts.

Students are often easily influenced by the adults in their lives. Unconsciously, boys and girls gather information, formulate their thoughts, and learn how to make their own decisions about right and wrong just by watching their world in action. Most of the time in that world, it's the parent's responsibility to teach values, morals, and the essence of right and wrong to their own children. Often enough though, the task of teaching those concepts falls upon the shoulders of grandparents and other extended family members.

In the end, however, we as counselors also have the opportunity to help children think for themselves when.it comes to applying all they have learned about right and wrong to the multitude of situations they will be faced with.

Student Reflection:

I went to counseling group today with our school counselor. The counselor usually calls my classroom once a week looking for me. Whenever the phone rings, I can't help to look up and see if my teacher looks my way. I can usually tell when it's Dr. Nick calling for me because my teacher looks at me and gets a big grin on her face!

Even though I knew everybody in my group today, we had to introduce each other! That was kind of fun because we usually introduce ourselves. I got to introduce my friend by telling his name, grade, and three positive words that I think describe the kind of person he is.

I felt pretty special when my friend talked about me. I had a great feeling hearing someone say nice stuff about me. It's way better hearing those nice things said by someone else, but Dr. Nick told me I should remember to say them to myself sometimes too.

After we did introductions, we only had time to talk about one thing from our week with family, school, or friends. I chose school. I told everyone that I had a great week in school so far. I've been coming to school pretty much on time, did most of my schoolwork, and only had to miss break twice in the last couple days.

The counselor thought I was doing much better and making good decisions more often than I used to make, but he also wanted to know why I missed break. I told him, "Well, my friend needed some help during these tests we were taking, so I passed him a note with the answers on them."

Dr. Nick said he liked that I've got a really good friendship, but he also said my friendship may have blocked me from seeing other important things too. I didn't really know what he was talking about, and I'm sure he could tell that by the look on my face. He told me we would talk about it later.

Our counselor gave everybody a sheet of paper. He asked that we draw two lines on it long ways, like from top to bottom to split the paper into three rows. We were asked to name the first row right, the middle row wrong, and the third row depends. This was pretty easy to do, but I also liked that he showed us how to do that with his own paper.

Dr. Nick told us he would be reading some numbered questions or statements one at a time. He said each question would have something to do with honesty, friendship, stuff we believe in, and other things too.

It was good that he gave us a practice question. He said, "Do you consider throwing out your parent's beer the right thing to do, the wrong thing to do, or would it depend?" Most of the kids made a huge inhaling sound when he asked that question!

We all had an answer, and everybody wanted to talk at the same time. Eventually everyone took a turn in giving an answer. Most of us thought throwing out our parent's beer was the right thing to do, but it's also not right to throw away something that doesn't belong to you. My dad and mom would kill me if I did that!

Dr. Nick said we were to write our answers on our paper by placing the number of the question in the row we felt was correct. Like, if question number one was the practice question he just gave us, we would place the number one in either the right, wrong, or depends row.

Even though I pretty much understood how he wanted me to write on my paper, I felt way more confident when I could see how he wanted us to do it on his own paper again. Once everybody knew what to do for sure, Dr. Nick read the following ten questions.

1. Is lying ever the right thing to do, the wrong thing to do, or does it depend?

2. Is taking something without permission the right thing to do, the wrong thing to do, or does it depend?

3. Is keeping something you found the right thing to do, the wrong thing to do, or does it depend?

4. Is cheating ever the right thing to do, the wrong thing to do, or does it depend?

5. Is remaining silent when knowing the answer to a question ever the right thing to do, the wrong thing to do, or does it depend?

6. Is allowing someone to be bullied the right thing to do, the wrong thing to do, or does it depend?

7. Is giving a beggar money ever the right thing to do, the wrong thing to do, or does it depend?

8. Is giving your friend an answer during a test ever the right thing to do, the wrong thing to do, or does it depend?

9. Is choosing fighting as a way to handle anger ever the right thing to do, the wrong thing to do, or does it depend?

10. Is telling the truth always the right thing to do, the wrong thing to do, or does it depend?

I thought some of these questions were easy and some were pretty hard. I was feeling frustrated because the more we talked and thought about the questions, the more harder the answers got!

The counselor also said that it's important to think about right and wrong because lots of people believe in right and wrong. Those people are like parents, grandparents, policemen, lawyers, jurors, doctors, the people that run juvy hall, and presidents. He said teachers believe in right and wrong too! That's when Dr. Nick looked at me. He said the reason I got in trouble and missed my break wasn't because I did the right thing and helped my friend, but because I did the right thing in the wrong way.

We got to talk about how sometimes a person has to first figure out that sometimes there might be more than one right thing to think about. Like how it's right to not cheat on a test, and it's also right to help a friend. Even once we figure out all the right things that are going on, we then have to figure out how to do it all the right way! Dr. Nick said that's what family, friends, teachers, and counselors are for.

Dr. Nick had us go over some of the questions from his list and think about what some of the right things are and some of the right ways to deal with them. That was pretty hard to do, and I know he said to ask our parents and grandparents about some of them.

We had to push our chairs in around the table as we left group, and our counselor gave everybody a little card to give to our parents. Written on the card was just one question with three answers our parents had to choose from. The question was, "Does right and wrong ever depend on the situation?" The answers were: yes, no, or depends.

Dr. Nick said to bring our cards back next week because he's really looking forward to hearing about the talks we'll have had with our folks. Besides, anyone who brings back the card would get a special award that reads, "Right makes Might!"

Dear Parent,

Your child's presence in counseling group today was appreciated! The counseling activity today was called: "Right, Wrong, or Depends." Students were read a list of situational questions. Each question addressed issues of values. For example, one question was, "Is telling the truth always the right thing to do, the wrong thing to do, or does it depend? Questions like this really got the group talking! Students were encouraged to discuss family values and the issues of right and wrong with their families.

SUPER HERO

Goal of Activity: To promote a greater understanding of the super hero concept and to encourage students to look to themselves and other members of their families in becoming everyday super heroes.

Student Mix: boys and girls of similar age and grade

Group Size: four to six students

Suggested Time: forty to forty-five minutes

Materials Required: comic books, masks, capes and props of super heroes, camera, sticky labels, and folders

Considerations:

Children possess an inherent need to have heroes in their lives. Boys and girls of all ages actively seek out heroes. More times than not, the search for heroes initially begins in their own homes.

Whether or not the heroes in their homes live up to the child's expectations, kids invariably will look to larger than life super heroes found in our culture. In a time where comic book heroes have come to life on film and their special abilities are dramatically magnified through the medium of special effects, student's expectations of their super heroes have also increased.

This activity helps to transform the concept of super hero back into something more manageable, reasonable, and practical for girls and boys to believe in. Through this activity, we as counselors can bring back into focus the original definition of what true heroes in our homes are really all about: keeping promises, maintaining friendships, and being responsible.

Student Reflection:

The call from the counselor came right on time today! Dr. Nick asked for me and another kid from my room to go to counseling group. I felt pretty important showing the new kid the way to the counselor's office.

I asked Dr. Nick if I could introduce my friend, Dillon, to the other kids in our group. I liked how I felt introducing him. I felt like I was the expert, and I liked how the other kids listened to me.

After everybody got introduced, we did check-in. We all took turns sharing something about our week with family, friendships, and school. The counselor also had us say who our favorite super heroes are and why! We were also asked to give our past week a score between one through ten. A low score meant we had a really hard or bad week. A high score would mean our week was awesome and things went really well. We also had to talk about why our week was good, bad, or somewhere in between.

This one boy sitting next to me gave his week a score of three. He told us that because the police came to his house on Tuesday night and took his dad to jail. Then, as the cops were backing out of the driveway, the police guy ran over his cat. We talked about Tanner's story for a pretty long time. We voted to see if his score of three was low enough. It wasn't.

I felt pretty excited as Dr. Nick began our counseling activity by sharing comic books with us! He told us to look through the pages and find any super heroes we thought were neat or just plain cool. Within a couple minutes everyone had found some super heroes to show and tell about. We then had to do two things. First, say why we chose that hero, and second, tell what makes that character so special.

Once everybody took their turn, Dr. Nick offered to help us become super heroes! He laid out several pieces of super hero costumes like masks, capes, shields, and other stuff like staffs, swords, and power bracelets. I got really wound up when he told us we could dress up like a super hero if we wanted to! Too cool! We could wear any parts of the costumes we chose as long as we put them on over our street clothes.

Dr. Nick told us we could invent our very own super hero names and come up with a list of our own super hero special powers! That's when he told us about the two things that every super hero has got to have so they can be a super hero. They're wanting to help others and the courage to see it through. By now everyone was getting way excited about becoming a super hero!

Once all of us knew what we wanted to be and how our costume would look, we had to figure out super hero names and what our super hero powers would be. Dr. Nick took pictures of us twice. Like, he took my picture as my regular self, and then he took my picture as a super hero. He then put both pictures in my very own folder. Everybody had their own folder that had their own super hero name and list of super powers.

Doing that was some of the most fun I've ever had in counseling! I loved getting dressed up like a super hero! Everyone seemed to be having as much fun as I was having. I loved it even more when Dr. Nick gave me my folder! There was a picture of me on the left side of the folder with my regular name just below my picture. On the right side of the folder was my super hero picture with my super hero name! I looked really cool!

After everyone had a chance to do like a show and tell about their folders, Dr. Nick said we could take them home and show them to our families. Just as I started to think that we were done for the day, Dr. Nick showed us a picture of one of his super heroes. Boy, was I ever surprised when he showed us a picture of some old guy in his seventies! I thought he must be joking! Dr. Nick said that the guy in the picture was his Super Grandpa!

Our counselor told us that real super heroes are promise keepers, friend makers, and responsibility takers. Heroes are also people we are proud of and want to be like. We talked for a little bit about what those things were all about.

Dr. Nick says that super heroes come in all shapes and sizes and usually wear everyday costumes like of moms, dads, grand-mas, grandpas, teachers, custodians, police, and firemen. He said that super heroes are polite, respectful, and can tackle any big things that stand in their way of becoming even more super! Just when I thought he was going to bust a gut, he kept talking and said, "Super heroes fight to do the right thing even though they're usually outnumbered and probably won't become popular with too many people around them!"

Wow! I've never seen Dr. Nick that excited before! I thought it was pretty funny that as he was saying all that stuff he was putting on a mask and cape and stood on a chair with his hands on his hips. That's when he gave each of us our very own sticky label. The sticky label read: "Promise Keeper, Friend Maker, and Responsibility Taker." The counselor had us place the label in our folders right below our super hero pictures and names.

Just before we left group, Dr. Nick said he really wants us to understand that we're already super heroes whether we're wearing a cape and mask or a backpack and mittens! He says that each of us has what it takes to become a super hero because of our wanting to help others and our courage to see it through.

Dear Parent,

Our counseling activity dealt with the concept of being a "Super Hero." Did you know that all super heroes share the desire of wanting to help others and that they also have the courage to accomplish their goals? Did you also know that "real" super heroes are promise keepers, friend makers, and responsibility takers? Just ask your child about the super heroes in his or her life. Moms, Dads, Teachers, Policemen, Brothers, and Sisters can all be the kind of super hero kids look up to.

SEQUENCE MAKES SENSE

Goal of Activity: To help the student understand that behavior is best understood in terms of the sequence of events in which the behavior occurs rather than as a single isolated event.

Student Mix: boys and girls of approximately the same age and grade

Size of Group: four to six students

Suggested Time: twenty to thirty minutes

Materials Required: pencils, papers, and treats

Considerations:

Students have a need to comprehend, in terms and images they already understand, the how and why events in their lives happen. On some deep level, in the absence of any understanding, kids will attempt to make sense of those events. Sometimes boys and girls will create their own realities to fill in the gaps that prevent them from fully understanding some of the events in their lives. Other times, however, boys and girls may inadvertently eliminate or compromise certain aspects of what they already understand in an attempt to make sense of a series of events they're confronted with.

On another more superficial level, students may be fully aware of their role in a series of events that have led up to a current situation they find themselves in. However, failure to take responsibility or ownership for their actions frequently plays out as either inaccurate sequencing or intentional disregard of specific information in the re-telling of those events.

Know, however, that girls and boys may either intentionally or unintentionally be inaccurate in their recount of certain events for a wide variety of reasons. Helping students understand how they sequence the events in their lives is what this activity hopes to address. However, helping students come to terms with understanding the why behind having sequenced certain experiences may be best left for individual sessions and another day.

Student Reflection:

We didn't have counseling group yesterday but we did have it today. My teacher told me first thing yesterday morning that our counselor wouldn't be at school. Even though I felt disappointed, I was still glad I found out early that he wouldn't be coming. I would have spent all day looking at the clock and wondering when my counselor would be calling me! Was I ever glad he called for me today!

During check-in when we were talking about our families, I saw Dr. Nick was trying to write down everybody's names that we talked about. I asked him what he was doing, and he told me he was trying to figure out how everybody is connected together in families. For example, he wrote down the name of my dad, mom, brothers, and sisters. He then drew a line that connected my dad's name to my mom's name. Then down under my parents' names, he had written the names of the kids in my family with lines connecting us all together.

Later, Dr. Nick said we needed to help him double-check all of the names on his list. Some of us have really big families with people scattered all over the place. This one girl has had like four different dads!

Once the double-checking was done, Dr. Nick told us to write the numbers one through ten in order and the letters of the alphabet in A through Z order on our own sheet of paper. The counselor then told everyone to erase any number and letter or mix around any number or letter on our paper.

He showed us how to do it, but I knew what he meant. What I did was switch the numbers two and nine around. Then I erased the letter F from my letters list. Once everyone had switched or erased a letter or number probably like I did, we traded papers with the person sitting next to us.

Dr. Nick then challenged us to figure out what the change was that our neighbor made to their paper. This took a little bit of time because we had to go over like every number and letter to make sure they were in order. After everyone finished correcting their paper, we gave them back to the person we got them from. It sounded like everyone done a pretty good job about finding out what was different or out of order.

Our counseling activity then got started with Dr. Nick showing us one little section of a cartoon sketch that didn't have any words written on it. It was just two little cavemen guys standing next to something that to me looked sort of like a rock. Dr. Nick said the picture came from an old b.c. comic strip. He then asked everyone to make up our own story about the sketch he showed us. I said, "I think the two guys are fighting over whose rock it is." Everyone took a turn at making up a story.

The counselor then showed us a second sketch that looked a lot like the first, but now one of the cavemen was standing there with a rock of his own. Dr. Nick told us to fix our story to fit in both pictures. I had to change my story a little bit and said, "The one guy is going to hit the other guy with a bigger rock." It took some time but everybody changed or fixed their story a little bit. This one kid had to change all of his story.

Dr. Nick showed us a third piece of the comic and asked that we fix our stories one more time to fit in the third drawing. Most kids had to change their stories a whole bunch, but one of the kid's stories just didn't make any sense at all. I just thought the two guys were just gathering rocks to start a rock war. The counselor then put all three sketches on the whiteboard in their right order. Snap! I was way off! They were building a snowman!

We did this same thing like three or four more times with different pieces of comic strips. I was starting to get pretty good at figuring out the right order of how the comic sections should go together. Like, once they were placed in the right order, they all made sense!

Dr. Nick went to the whiteboard and wrote, "Events make sense when they're in sequence." The counselor said that lots of things we do or have done can make sense when they're placed in a sequence things like getting a book, opening the book, reading the book, and then telling about the book. He also said like how sometimes people want to erase or switch things around in their lives, kinda like what we did with the numbers and letters at the beginning of our group.

He then told us about this one boy he knew who wanted to forget that his dad had died. The boy sometimes still pretends his father is alive but just on vacation. He also told us about a girl he used to know a long time ago who wanted to forget about some-thing she saw her uncle do that wasn't very nice.

A couple of the kids in our group didn't say anything but did shake their heads up and down. Dr. Nick asked if they wanted to say anything. One of the girls who nodded told about how she sometimes leaves out certain stuff from her stories when she has to talk to the principal. The girl said something like the principal usually doesn't believe her because the principal told her, "Your story doesn't make any sense, what haven't you told me?" I accidentally blurted out, "That sounds just like my dad!" I covered my mouth and said no more after that.

I thought about telling Dr. Nick about the time some friends and I were out throwing rocks at cars. One rock I threw hit a car as it was driving by, and I broke its windshield. The car ran into a tree. We all ran as fast as we could. The police showed up at my house like the next day, but I told them a lie about where I was and who I was with. The officer told me my story didn't make much sense and just kept staring at me. When the policeman left, my dad told me he didn't believe me either.

Dr. Nick told us that counseling can help people become okay with some of parts of their lives that they might like to forget or reorder. He said that learning how to make sense of things is one of the biggest reasons a person might go to see a counselor someday!

If I keep thinking about this rock thing much longer, I think I'll tell him about it next week because it really bugs me, and I think about it like all the time!

When we were getting out of group today, Dr. Nick told me to stop back sometime, and maybe he could help me out a little bit with getting my dad to believe me again. He said even though it's hard sometimes to put things in their right order, I'll be able to move on and just forget about those things and so will my dad.

That's what I want to do.

Dear Parent,

Boys and girls can sometimes get their facts out of order when re-telling important events. Often bits of information are left out or jumbled around to make the story sound different than it really happened. That may happen for a variety of reasons. The counseling activity today focused on the importance of telling the exact sequence of how events have unfolded. When a boy or girl tells the whole story in the sequence in which the story occurred, the story just makes better sense.

ROUND AND ROUND WE GO

Goal of Activity: To help the student broaden his or her understanding of the relationship between individual behavior and group image.

Student Mix: boys and girls of similar age and grade

Group Size: five to six students

Suggested Time: thirty to forty minutes

Materials Required: die (one dice), paper numbers, whistle, certificates, tape, and treats

Considerations:

This activity is intended to help boys and girls to be mindful of maintaining their individual sense of self and responsibilities within the confines of group behavior. Students lacking in sufficient ego strength or self-esteem often tend to forget themselves when they are under the influence of their assorted peer groups. These children are often the first ones to adopt group mentality as their own.

In the absence of strong positive group leadership, many boys and girls choose to take the fast track in securing an identity as representatives of their group. Quite often, however, the immediate payoff of securing an instant identity results in poor judgment and misbehavior. This fast path to becoming "somebody," although well intended but somewhat misguided, will actually further delay the student from establishing a better and broader sense of self.

As counselors, we have the opportunity to create positive group experiences for the kids who participate in our groups. These group experiences not only allow students to improve their self-esteem, but they also serve to nurture the development of positive individual leadership skills within, and as representatives of the their groups.

Student Reflection:

I sat in class waiting for our counselor to call me. He usually calls for me about the same time each week for group. I was getting pretty restless and didn't get any work done for a pretty long time. My teacher noticed I wasn't doing anything and told me I would have to get my work done first, even if the counselor called right now! That really made me mad! When the phone in my room rang, I heard my teacher say, "Could I send her after she finishes her science paper?"

I nearly threw a fit when I heard her say that! My teacher did tell me that Dr. Nick had said, "School comes first, send her as soon as she's done." Crap! That sounds exactly like something he would say. I've heard him say that on the phone before when I've been in his office.

When I finally got to counseling group, I didn't recognize anybody! These kids were all older than me! Dr. Nick introduced me, and I sat down next to this other girl. She looked at me kind of funny, rolled her eyes, and slid her chair away from me. I wasn't liking this new group so much, and I felt like blaming my teacher on making me miss my regular group.

Even though this was a new group for me, our group started with check-in just like my usual group does. Dr. Nick asked everyone only like once or twice during check-in about how we felt about different things going on in our lives with family, school, and friendships.

The one thing I noticed Dr. Nick do differently with the older kids during check-in was that he had them, as a group, earn a treat for having a good check-in. Having a good check-in meant everyone had to avoid saying fewer than five word answers when asked about family, school, and friends. For example, if someone said, "My family is fine," no one in group would earn a treat for check-in! Double crap! I'm glad he doesn't do that in my group. We would all starve to death!

The counselor leaned over and told me the reason he has the five word minimum rule is because he wants kids to really think about what's going on at home, in school, and with their friend-ships. He said because anything less than five important words doesn't really explain very much. I think Dr. Nick is way harder on these older kids than he is with me and the kids in my usual group.

When check-in was over, Dr. Nick made this announcement that we would be doing an activity called "Save the group."

Dr. Nick got the activity started by telling us to move our chairs, facing them outwards in the shape of a circle. There were chairs for everyone in the group. Each chair had a number taped on the back of it. We were told to walk clockwise around the outside of the circle of chairs until we heard a whistle blow. As soon as we heard the sound of the whistle, we were to sit down fast in the first open chair. The counselor said there would be no pushing or shoving because there are chairs for everybody, and he wants everyone to be safe.

The counselor then rolled one dice. If the number on the dice matched the number of the chair we were sitting in, we were called on to save the group. Whoever the kid sitting in that chair was, that kid would have to answer a question the counselor would ask. Dr. Nick said the questions might be about something social that includes lots of people or something personal that might just be about one person.

Like two questions he asked were: "Who is most responsible for the trash on our school campus? And, "What are some thoughts you might have if you knew your friend was cheating on a history test?"

Dr. Nick scored answers with a number between one and fifteen. He said that low scores showed low effort and not too much thought. High scores meant you gave a really good answer that took lots of effort and good thinking.

The questions Dr. Nick had asked were:

Who is most responsible for the trash on our school campus?

What are some thoughts you might have if you knew your friends were cheating on a history test?

There is a group of six students, four of the students are teasing two younger kids on the playground. What do you think of that group's behavior?

The neighborhood kids you're with begin making bad hand signs at the drivers of cars as they drive by. What do you think the driver of the car thinks about the kids who are in that group?

Someone in your group of friends at school was accused of stealing ice cream from the lunch room. You know who really stole the ice cream. What do you do if none of your other friends are saying anything?

You are asked to represent your team at an out of school event at the mall. How might you act?

You were placed on a relay race team with three other students from your class. Two of the three students are not trying their best. What do you say or do?

Three of the kids in your group of friends at school have knives in their backpacks. You don't. Do you do anything?

You are at a birthday party and some members of your group dare you to do something foolish and dangerous. What do you do?

A fire breaks out in your home and everyone other than you begins to panic. How do you save the group?

After everybody in our group was given a question to answer and it was scored, Dr. Nick figured out what our group score was. If the total group score was higher than all of our ages added together, we would be winners in saving the group.

Well, this worked out pretty good. I know I had some pretty good answers, and I'm also a couple years younger than all of the other kids in group. Our total group score for the six of us was sixty-nine! When we added all of our ages together, we came up with just sixty-seven. We saved the group!

Dr. Nick gave everybody a congratulations card. I was feeling like I had done pretty good and even that one girl who didn't like me so much at the beginning of group told me I had done a good job! I felt great, I felt like I fit in!

After all the cards were handed out, the counselor talked about how important group behavior and group image is. Like, he said that image is about what we might look like and act like to other people if they were noticing us.

He reminded us that no matter what group we're in whether it's our family group, school group, or our group of friends, it only takes one person to make a positive difference. In fact, enough of a difference that it just might save the group, like it did today in our game.

Dr. Nick told us about a group of kids he knows from the high school. He said he had seen the kids hanging out together at the mall this past weekend. All of the kids were dressed in the same type of clothing, jewelry, and hair styles. Some of the kids even had tattoos on their arms and knuckles. Dr. Nick said they may have looked very suspicious to other people.

Well, it turns out that one of the kids in the group ended up helping a little girl find her mom! Dr. Nick said that when the mom turned around and saw her daughter holding the hand of the one kid with tattoos on his arms and pants sagging down to his knees, she was speechless! Dr. Nick had overheard the mom say to the high school kid, "You and your friends just don't look like the type of people who would do something so nice."

We spent the next couple minutes talking about the questions Dr. Nick had given us during our game. I didn't know it at the time he first asked, but I think all of those questions had something to do with group things.

I liked that he wanted to know what everyone's most interesting question was from the list. He also said we had to tell him why we chose the question we picked. Not only that, we also had to tell him about why our age might be an important part of the question we picked. For sure he makes the older kids in this group think harder, but you know what? I think I handled it pretty good.

Leaving group today, Dr. Nick told everyone to keep putting lots of effort and thought into what they do when they're out with friends and family. He also told us to get our friends and family to do their best too when we're all out together doing stuff because, even though it only takes one person to save the group, it only takes one person to give everybody in that group a bad image.

Dear Parent,

The counseling activity today explored appropriate ways of dealing with pressures that boys and girls often feel in conforming to the verbal and non-verbal demands of their peers. Students in group were presented with a variety of situational questions that required their responses. Whenever a student could successfully identify the source of the pressures found in the question and counter with an appropriate response for dealing with those pressures, that student would thus "Save the group."

POPSICLE STICK

Goal of Activity: To help the student improve his or her understanding of how relationships can be damaged, broken, repaired, and maintained.

Student Mix: boys and girls of similar age and grade

Group Size: four to six students

Suggested Time: thirty to forty minutes

Materials Required: popsicle sticks and tape

Considerations:

Relationships are hard to understand. The guidelines for building and maintaining relationships are seldom well defined. Growing up and going through school are often the playing fields where boys and girls practice the ongoing cycle of establishing, developing, maintaining, repairing, and sometimes scrapping relationships.

Children need to learn how to repair broken relationships with their families and friends. Saying sorry is seldom ever enough to repair a relationship but it is a good start.

Essentially, the goal in this lesson is to help kids think of their relationships in terms of something that binds one person to another. The activity uses the wheel concept and popsicle sticks to help make this point.

Getting students to use their imagination is easy. Getting them to understand that the invisible connection they have with another person is real may be the biggest goal to achieve. As a counselor, you will want to develop your skills in learning how to superimpose concepts onto things that students can see, feel, and understand. Remember, a student's success in knowing how to develop relationships is contingent upon your ability to communicate with the student in terms the student can identify with.

Student Reflection:

I went to counseling this afternoon. Dr. Nick, our school counselor, came to my classroom, opened the door, and looked inside. The teacher saw him and then looked at me. I like how I feel when I'm sent to go with our counselor. I think most of the other kids think I'm important and lucky. A couple of the kids might think I'm weird, but I don't really care.

On our way over to the counselor's office, we stopped by a couple classrooms to get the other kids from our group. It's fun poking my head inside everyone's classroom to see what they're doing too, but Dr. Nick asked me to stand back away from the door. He said he doesn't want to disrupt the classrooms any more than necessary because the teachers are trying to teach. That made sense, but I still wanted to look into the other classrooms.

By the time we got to Dr. Nick's office, everyone seemed ready to get started with group. Today Dr. Nick asked that we sign our names on his group sheet. That was new, but we all signed in anyway.

Our group began as it usually does with check-in. During check-in, Dr. Nick gets most kids to talk about something important about their past week with family, at school, and with friends. I noticed something else that was different during check-in. Dr. Nick used the sign-in sheet to copy our names onto the whiteboard. He also wrote down the names of any family member or friend we talked about.

How he wrote down our names was pretty neat. Like, he put my name in the center of something that reminded me of a wheel or circle. He put the names of my family members and friends around and outside of the wheel. When I got finished with my part of check-in, Dr. Nick drew connecting lines from the center of the circle where my name was to each surrounding name. It looked just like a big bicycle wheel! Cool! The counselor did this for everybody in group. The whiteboard was covered with bicycle wheels! Once we all had a wheel of our own, Dr. Nick had us get ready for the counseling activity.

Everyone was given four popsicle sticks. The counselor told us to write number one on one of the sticks, number two on another stick, number three on another stick, and number four on the last stick. We were told to lay the sticks on the tabletop directly in front of where we were sitting down at. Dr. Nick then asked us to think of three different ways a popsicle stick could be broken. Everybody shouted out answers, but he pretended he didn't hear them. He only called on a person if that person had their hand in the air. I guess that got everybody to raise their hands. I think the answers I heard most were snapping the sticks with your hands, chopping them with an ax, and cutting the sticks with a saw.

Dr. Nick then made his voice sound really important and said that stick number one would not be hurt. Stick number two would get snapped in half. Stick number three would be snapped in two places, and stick number four would be broken in three or more places!

I noticed right away that some kids loved doing stick breaking.

It was good that Dr. Nick brought some extra sticks because two kids in our group started breaking other kid's sticks! I was thinking I was just about ready to use one of my sticks to poke this kid who was trying to break my number one stick, but the counselor said something about me maybe being safer in the principal's office. He said I got one more chance.

Once we had our sticks snapped and lined up in order on the table in front of us, we were asked to think of ways we could fix the broken sticks, just in case we had to. Everybody got called on again to give answers, and the counselor wrote our answers on his paper. Super gluing, taping, and cementing were the favorite things kids said to do.

Dr. Nick only had tape for everybody to use and challenged us to repair our busted sticks. Some sticks were easier to fix than others. I saw that some of the sticks that had lots of breaks were super hard to fix, and I think some sticks just couldn't be fixed at all.

After like a couple minutes, the counselor told us to stop trying to fix the sticks and look back to the circles on the white-board. He pointed to the lines or spokes on the wheels and said the spokes are kinda like connections we have with those different people. He also said that everyone on our wheel is important because that's why we talked about them.

Dr. Nick told us that connections are also called relationships and that's what connects two people together. When the connection is good, the stick is unbroken or has been fixed so that it's as good as new. He also said that things like lying, cheating, and breaking promises are just like snapping, axing, and cutting popsicle sticks.

The counselor looked at each of our wheels on the white-board. He could see that a couple kids in our group live in two different houses. He really wanted those kids to keep or fix their connections with their parents, even though their moms and dads connection with each other might be busted really, really bad, like in a million pieces!

I looked at my wheel on the whiteboard and started thinking about my own parents not living together anymore. I didn't want anyone to know about my dad having a girlfriend. That's why I didn't mention her name during check-in, even though I see her all the time. Was I ever surprised when the counselor told us of a secret wish many boys and girls have. The wish he says is that lots of kids want their parents to get back together! How does he know what I'm thinking!

Dr. Nick then reminded us that just like stick number four, sometimes if the connection between our moms and dads is really messed up, maybe it's just best to leave it alone because it can't be fixed and still be any good. I liked that he told us that even if our connection with someone is broken and really messed up, we could still save a good memory from before the connection with that person got broken. Dr. Nick said everything that happens is going to be a memory one day anyway, so why not just keep it a good memory.

Dr. Nick asked us all to look at our wheels on the whiteboard and to think about how our connections with those people are. He asked that we think of the following questions as we look at each name on our wheels.

Who are our unbroken relationships with?

Which relationships have we glued back together?

Which connections are we still working on?

Do we have any relationships that aren't fixable?

Dr. Nick told us that if we ever want to fix connections that are still fixable, we should try and use things like patience, effort, honesty, and forgiveness instead of stuff like super glue, tape, and cement. He told us he would gladly help us fix any of those relationships if we wanted him to.

Dr. Nick gave a brand new popsicle stick to all the kids who said they have a broken connection with somebody on their wheel. He told us to take the stick home, write that person's name on it, keep it safe, and keep working at keeping it strong. He also gave everybody a new popsicle stick who lives in two different houses too. He told us that maybe we can use the stick for any new people we get to have in our lives. I asked him if I could poke that new person with it. He got a pretty big grin on his face and said that's not quite exactly what he meant. We both laughed!

Dear Parent,

The counseling activity today was all about relationships. In the activity, popsicle sticks were used to help students visually understand how relationships are often felt. An unbroken stick is much like a great relationship. A broken stick represents a relationship that has been damaged by any number of means. Some sticks were broken but have sense been mended. Be sure to ask your child about the sticks he or she identified as being whole, broken, mended, or damaged beyond repair in his or her life.

TOUGH CHANGE

Goal of Activity: The student will begin to learn how to transform burdensome experiences into experiences that are emotionally more productive and manageable.

Student Mix: boys and girls of similar age and grade

Group Size: four to six students

Suggested Time: thirty-five to forty minutes

Materials Required: magic box, container of coins, a $100 bill, and a CD player with just the right assortment of songs and inspirational lyrics

Considerations:

This lesson really underscores the importance of encouraging students to actively seek help in their pursuit of tackling issues that continue to weigh heavily in their hearts and minds.

Using the concept of magic often gets the children's interest right away. Keeping their interest, however, is the real trick. Remember, you don't need to be a great magician to pull this activity off. All you really need is a jar of coins, a large enough cash bill to get their attention, and a box with a divider in the middle with a dual lid that hinges in its center. Better yet, it's probably best just to devise your own magic box.

Know that you won't always have the right words to say when you think the student needs to hear just the right thing. Sometimes the best things we can say will be those magic phrases that are meant to encourage and support students in their discovery of answers to questions only they will eventually find.

Student Reflection:

I didn't know two of the kids in my counseling group today, but after introductions and check-in, I felt like I knew a little bit about them. I think it's easier for me to talk about myself when I know who the people in my group are.

Our group got started with Dr. Nick having us sit in order of our heights. Like, we had to have the shortest person in the group sitting in the chair to his left side. Sitting to the left of that girl was the next tallest person, and that kept happening all the way around the table until the tallest kid was sitting in the chair over by Dr. Nick's right hand.

For check-in, Dr. Nick wanted everybody to try and think about anything we've been part of that's been really hard or tough to deal with. Like, it might be something from last year or even something that's happening right now. Dr. Nick said it could even be something that's going to happen pretty soon!

He gave an example of something that happened to him last year. He told us about when his dog ran away from home, and he still misses him! He even showed us the picture of his dog that he keeps in his pocket. Now I knew what he was talking about when he talked about hard things to deal with.

The shortest girl in our group said she might be going to Missouri to live with her dad. This pretty tall kid said something about his brother's funeral like three or four years ago. The tallest kid, named Brandon, still remembers the day his hamster crawled into their dryer and tumbled dried to death! Gross! He said the lint catcher was full of hamster fluff! Really gross!

I was pretty surprised to hear how much stuff most of the kids wanted to say about all those things. There were so many! Dr. Nick gave everyone a treat for doing such a great job talking about some really hard things.

Our counselor started our activity by putting a big jar of change on the table in front of us. There must have been over a thousand coins in that jar! One kid who got to hold the jar said it must have weighed like twenty pounds! Dr. Nick told us he used to carry lots of this change in his pants pocket but pretty soon couldn't anymore because it got to be too heavy. No kidding!

He looked pretty sad when he was telling us about all the change he had to carry for a long time. The way he said it made me feel a little sorry for him. One of the kids asked him why he kept so much change with him for so long, and Dr. Nick said he didn't know what else to do with it until his friend, Lowell, showed him a really cool magic trick. I love magic! Everyone wanted him to show us what the magic trick was.

Dr. Nick put the change jar into a big cardboard box. He covered the box with a cloth. He then spun the box around and around while saying magic phrases that hardly anybody else could hear.

As soon as he tapped his ruler on the box, he took the rag off the top of it. He opened the box lid and the coins were gone! He pulled out a hundred dollar bill! That was awesome! Everybody wanted it! Even though everybody wanted the money, Dr. Nick said he's the one who is supposed to carry it.

For fun, Dr. Nick said he was going to turn the money back into all that change. He placed the hundred dollar bill back into the box, covered the box with a cloth, spun the box around in the other direction, hit the box with the ruler, and then showed us the jar of coins!

We were all still pretty amazed, but I was also starting to get a little suspicious. I wanted to look closer at that magic box, but the counselor kept me back. He said something about that believing is sometimes better than knowing. Our counselor then put the coin jar on our table. He said he wanted to show us some of the coins he had been keeping for all of those years.

Dr. Nick held up a nickel and asked us what it was. Brandon shouted out, "A nickel!" Dr. Nick said, "Well, it is a nickel, but it's also the time my family moved to a new town." He then held up a quarter and pointed to a girl who wasn't shouting and asked her what it was. The girl answered, "A quarter." "Yes, it is a quarter," said Dr. Nick, "but it's also the time my parents divorced."

The counselor then showed us a silver dollar and asked us to name it. Before anyone shouted out an answer, we talked first. One kid said it was a silver dollar and guessed that it was also something worser than his parents divorcing. We were right! Dr. Nick told us that the coin was about the time his grandmother died.

Dr. Nick told us that no matter how short, tall, big, or small we are, we all have change that we carry around with us all the time. A couple kids emptied their pockets and said they didn't have any change, but one kid did show us his pocket knife. Dr. Nick asked to hold the knife until after school.

The counselor went back and talked about some of the things we had talked about during check-in, like the girl who might move to Missouri. We had to think about how that could work out to be a good change for her. Meeting new friends, spending more time with her dad, having snow in the winter, and hanging out with her cousins could all be great changes for her!

For that one kid whose brother died, that was way harder

to figure out. Dr. Nick said that the two of them could probably figure out a way the boy could learn how to sometimes celebrate his brother's life instead of always being sad and missing him. Dr. Nick said that for some things like when somebody dies or bad things happen to neat kids and their families, some magic is just harder to learn than others.

After Dr. Nick gave everyone a couple coins for the changes we had talked about having to carry, he put those three coins he used to tell us about himself back into his own pocket. I got it now what he meant when he said that each one of us has our own change to carry! I really got it this time!

I was glad when the counselor taught us some magic phrases to use if we ever feel like all the changes we sometimes have to carry are getting too heavy. He said magic phrases can help us turn sad, worried, and scary things into thoughts and feelings that are a lot easier to think about and carry phrases like: "I won't back down," "Don't worry, be happy," "I've got the eye of the tiger," "I think it's about forgiveness even if you don't love me anymore," "On the wings of eagles I can find my strength," "When a problem comes along you must whip it, whip it good," "I believe it's time for me to fly," "Hakuna matata," and "The Lord is my shepherd, I shall not want."

Dr. Nick said that some counselors, teachers, and parents are experts at knowing and saying magic things, and if we ever need any help, just to ask one of them. The counselor had written just some of those phrases on the whiteboard, and I had a lot of fun practicing saying those things out loud, over and over with the other kids in group. It felt like we were all chanting things at the same time and made it feel like all those phrases were really powerful!

Those were all pretty good magic phrases, but my favorite phrase was one our counselor used from a song he played on his CD player. I think he said the song was called, "Don't Stop Believing."

Dr. Nick told us any magic phrase we use will work better when we add lots of effort and positive thoughts in turning our change into something easier to deal with. "After all," said Dr. Nick, "it's a lot easier to carry a hundred dollar bill in your pocket than a hundred dollars worth of change."

Dear Parent,

In counseling group today, your child participated in an activity called "Tough Change." The activity was designed to help kids learn to deal more effectively with some of the "harder" changes they've experienced in their lives. In the example today, the counselor "magically" turned a jar of change into a hundred dollar bill! The real magic, however, occurred when the kids began turning some of their own tough changes in life into something a little easier to carry too!

THE PUZZLE

Goal of Activity: To help the student learn to deal more effectively and appropriately with the perceived and actual losses in his or her life

Student Mix: boys and girls of approximately the same age and grade

Group Size: four students

Suggested Time: twenty-five to thirty-five minutes

Materials Required: four twenty-five-piece puzzles and sticky notes

Considerations:

Children have a hard time moving forward when they feel something in their life is missing. Too often the void they feel becomes filled with anger, resentment, bitterness, or worse yet, apathy and denial. This is a good activity because it helps the counselor teach a lesson that addresses the issues of loss, grief, and adjustment.

As a reminder, be careful when you go poking around the empty places in a young person's heart. Even though boys and girls would have us believe their empty spaces are nothing more than dead zones no longer cared for, tend first to believe that they are simply lightly covered, wounds that never had the opportunity to properly mend.

Student Reflection:

My mom told me I had to go see the school counselor today. She thinks I have a bad attitude. When this counselor guy showed up to my classroom looking for me, I really thought, "This is going to be stupid."

The counselor introduced himself to me, but I didn't shake his hand. I told him straight out that I didn't want to be here and that the only reason I came with him is because my mom would take away my cell phone if I didn't. The counselor, "Dr. Nobody," told me I made the right decision considering how much I value the phone. What does he know about me anyway?

Three other kids came into the room I was in. They looked like they were glad to be here. What's up with that?

"Dr. Whatever" had us introduce ourselves. Then he wanted to know about goals we've been working on. I knew this was going to be lame. I told them the only goal I have is to keep my phone.

The counseling dude said we weren't going to be doing check-in today. That's good because I don't need to be checking-in with anybody. Instead he asked each of us, "Have you ever felt empty inside?" Are you kidding me? This was starting to sound like one of those really bad episodes of "Oprah."

One girl said she felt empty because she didn't have break-fast. Ha! I thought that was way funny and was glad she said something that would make him think he's not so smart. The counselor guy said the type of emptiness he was talking about was more like a feeling of missing something or someone. He then gave some examples of missing a dead person or a pet or something.

I actually stopped listening to what he was saying after he said feeling empty. Everyone else though had something to say, and I didn't like that the counselor was writing down their answers.

"Dr. Phil-Wannabe" gave us each like a twenty-five-piece puzzle to work on. He also gave us like only five minutes to get them done. I thought this was really going to be lame, but I also noticed the other kids were doing it. I thought then that maybe I'd put my puzzle together just to pass the time.

After a couple minutes, I knew without a doubt this was going to be a rip-off! Everyone, including me, was missing a piece of puzzle! I bet the stupid counselor lost them. He tried to cover up his goof by saying the missing pieces were probably just misplaced. He also asked a question about if the puzzles were still worth having even though they're missing a piece. My answer was, "No way!" The other kids thought their puzzles were still okay to have even if one piece was gone.

The counselor guy then showed everyone the note stickers he had been working on at the beginning of group when they were talking about the people, places, or things they missed. I saw that the note stickers were in the same shapes as the pieces of puzzle the other kids and me were missing.

The counselor gave one guy in our group a note sticker with the word "uncle" written on it and asked him to put it in the place of his missing puzzle piece. It fit just like the real piece of puzzle would have!

He gave a note sticker to a girl in our group with the word "grandma" printed on it, and another student received a note sticker with the word "hometown." Everybody got asked to put the note sticker they got into their empty puzzle space.

The counselor then showed us other same shaped note stickers with words like drugs, anger, gambling, gangs, depression, and suicide written on them. He said something about when a person is missing something or somebody then sometimes those people might try to fill up those empty spots with other things like the ones he just showed us.

Even though I pretty much got what he was saying, I didn't want him to think I was listening, so I just sat there and said, "This is stupid!"

Right about then, the counselor gave me a piece of sticky paper in the shape of the puzzle piece I was missing. On the paper was the word "dad." He asked me to place the sticker on my puzzle. I wouldn't do it, but he did. That's when he told me that some kids have a hard time learning how to deal with or get used to missing puzzle pieces.

I didn't look at him because I was feeling mad, sad, and I also felt like running out of that room and as far away as I could go. Dr. Nick told me he knew about my dad having gone to war two years ago and that the cell phone was the only connection I had left with him. Dr. Nick asked me when the last time my dad had called me and I told him, "Last year." Somehow I think the counselor guessed I probably call him every day. He was right.

I was feeling kind of okay that Dr. Nick told me he wanted to talk with me by myself about what's going on with me and my family, but I didn't want him to know I was feeling okay about that. I sat in group with my head sort of down for the next few minutes. I didn't know how to look at the other kids, actually, I wasn't sure what they would see if they looked at me.

I felt less pressure when the counselor took his stupid stare off me and told us how adults sometimes feel when they have a piece of puzzle missing. Dr. Nick said when parents feel a loss of a husband or wife, they may sometimes rush to replace that person with a new wife or a new husband. He also said that replacing someone doesn't always make things better, sometimes things get worse. The kid next to me said, "That's exactly what happened to my mom! That's why I have a jerk for a step dad. Even my mom can't stand him anymore!"

Instead of filling our empty puzzle space with something or someone else, Dr. Nick asked us to think about saving the empty space in our puzzle as a way to honor the something or someone we miss. He also said we could fill the space with good memories for comfort now and later use those memories when we feel like we might need courage and strength.

Before we left counseling group today, Dr. Nick told everyone to keep their missing puzzle piece. He said, "Just because we can't see or touch someone anymore doesn't mean we can't visualize or feel their presence."

He then had us close our eyes and remember the features of the person or places we were missing. For me, I imagined my dad's smile, the shape of his nose, the whiskers on his face, and the smell of his after shave. I also remembered our last Christmas together and the day he told me goodbye.

Dr. Nick had us sit in our chairs for a couple minutes just remembering that kind of stuff before we left group. I was starting to feel like I wanted to use my phone and call my dad. I really wanted to tell him about what happened in counseling group today, but I don't think I can reach him that way anymore but I'm going to keep trying.

Dear Parent,

Have you ever had a puzzle with one or two pieces missing? That's exactly what happened in group today! Your child had to make a decision about what to do with the empty space in his or her puzzle. The counseling lesson today dealt with the issue of personal loss. Through things like death, divorce, or changes in health and re-location, loss is experienced. How to deal appropriately with the emptiness that loss often creates became the question your child was helped to find answers to.

RISKY BUSINESS

Goal of Activity: To help the student understand the relationship between the concepts of chance and risk as it applies to the practice of everyday decision making.

Student Mix: boys and girls of similar age and grade

Group Size: six to eight students

Suggested Time: forty to fifty minutes

Materials Required: a slightly elevated balance beam

Considerations:

It's never too early or too late to help children learn about consequences of behavior. This activity seeks to broaden the student's awareness in understanding the breadth of those consequences.

There will never be a shortage of students who are placed in counseling services by teachers and parents with issues of impulsive behavior. Quite often, many of these boys and girls are the ones with attention deficit and hyperactivity related concerns. Keep in mind that as helpful as some medications are for treating attention deficit disorders, as of this time, there are no cures for any of those conditions. Boys and girls still need to learn how to think through a variety of situations and potential outcomes.

This can be a long mental activity to conduct. Considering you will have children in your group that experience great difficulties harnessing and sustaining their concentration and motor activity to begin with, you may wish to consider dividing this activity into a two-part lesson. As far as a balance beam goes, PVC pipe works just as well as an eight foot long two by four but you must make sure the ends are secure and the pipe does not roll under your student's feet. As in all activities you do, always think safety first.

Student Reflection:

Dr. Nick came by my classroom today and sat in the back of the room for a while before we went to counseling group. He told me that every now and then he visits with my teacher about my grades and how I behave in school. I feel kind of nervous not knowing what he's being told. I bet I could explain what I've done if I had to! My teacher says I always have a reason for everything!

We walked around to more classrooms and found the other kids in our group. When we finally got to his office, I think we were all surprised that the chairs and tables in his office were gone! Dr. Nick told us that we were going to take a chance and not use the tables and chairs today. I had the feeling this was going to be fun! I started running around the room like an airplane!

We had to sit on the floor, legs crossed, in the shape of a circle for check-in. We took turns talking about stuff going on in our families, with our friends, and how school was going.

This part of group is always so boring and takes forever! I undid my legs and started to bounce them up and down on the floor. I didn't have to go bathroom or anything so the counselor made me sit back down the way everybody else was.

I was still feeling a little nervous about what my teacher could have told Dr. Nick about my behavior in school. When it was my turn to talk about family, school, and friends, I sort of skipped over the school part. I was really glad when no one noticed!

Our counseling activity started with Dr. Nick asking, "Do you consider yourself someone who likes to take chances?" Everyone except this one weird girl in our group said they love taking chances. I stood up, held both my arms up, and started jumping up and down yelling "Me first, me first."

We were then told that everyone who answered yes to that first question automatically answers yes to the second question. That was so not fair, I couldn't believe it! I also couldn't believe it when Dr. Nick reminded me that I'm one of the kids in group that likes to take chances. He tricked me so it wasn't my fault!

With that, the one girl who said no to the counselor's first question, Dr. Nick asked her the second question, "Are you willing to risk your lunch today?"

In the next part of our activity, Dr. Nick sort of dared us, or what he said challenged us to walk across a really long, skinny board he had turned into a balance beam. He said if anyone could walk along the skinny side of the board from one end to the other, without falling, running, jumping, or touching the walls, floors, or another person, would earn a first in line lunch pass. Sweet!

Then he said if anyone who tries to walk across the balance beam and fails, that person would lose his or her lunch privilege for the day. The only other choice we had was not to do it. Too simple! Everyone in our group chose to do the dare, even the dorky girl who waited to hear what the second question was wanted to do it too.

I was so ready to walk across the balance beam. I knew I could do it. When it was my turn, I stepped up on the board, made sure everybody was looking at me, and kept telling myself that if I just go fast enough I can...#%✿●✿!

Dr. Nick thought it would be good if I apologized for using a bad word in group today. I did apologize, but I also know my parent's don't care if I say swear words as long as they're not too bad and they don't hear me say them. If I do get busted for saying the "F" word, I just have to tell the people I'm in trouble with that I forgot to take my medicine that day. Works every time!

Only one kid in our group made it across the balance beam without being disqualified. It was the stupid girl who earned the first in line lunch pass. She's the one who didn't want to do it in the first place! The rest of us lost our chance to eat lunch with the other kids! I was so mad, and this whole stinking thing was so unfair!

The counselor wanted us to go back to our sitting spots on the floor and talk about the activity, but I wanted to try it one more time. Dr. Nick insisted I follow directions, otherwise I wouldn't be able to finish the activity.

We sat on the floor, and I told everybody about how unfair this stupid thing was. The counselor asked if I wanted to look up the word fair in his special dictionary. I just rolled my eyes because his dictionary says it's not a real word.

Dr. Nick wrote the word "risk" on the whiteboard. He explained risk as being things that can be gotten or lost through something called "chance." He told us to think of chance as a behavior like walking across the balance beam and risk as a treasure that would be like our lunch. He said that behavior can get, keep, or take away any of our treasures or things we value.

Dr. Nick then gave an example of petting a stray dog. He asked two questions: "Who in this room would be willing to take a chance and pet a stray growling pit bull?" He then said that petting is the chance behavior. "If you answered yes to question number one, what treasures are you risking by taking that chance?" I wasn't surprised that some kids said they would pet the dog. I would too because I know the dog wants to be petted.

On the whiteboard, the counselor had written the names of ten risk areas that he called treasures. This is what he wrote:

1. Self-Image (how we want to be seen and known).

2. Reputation (how other people actually see and know us).

3. Self-Esteem (how we feel about ourselves).

4. Health and Safety Issues.

5. Relationships (connections with family teachers, and friends).

6. Money Things.

7. Legal Problems.

8. School Stuff.

9. Survival Concerns.

10. My Future.

Once he explained each thing and everybody sort of understood what they were, he then told us about ten situations that involved kids taking chances.

One by one, he read those situations out loud and asked us to figure out the treasures we could be risking in each situation. For example, the first situation was about a student thinking about taking his chances on forging his parents' name on his progress report. Dr. Nick said it this way, "Will taking the chance of forging, be worth the possible risks of ruining any of these treasures, like self-image?" Dr. Nick asked that question for each of the treasures he had pointed out on the whiteboard.

The other real life situations with chance-taking behaviors Dr. Nick talked about were:

Lying to a parent or teacher

Stealing from a friend

Cheating during a test

"One time" drug use

Running away from home

Dropping out of high school

Getting a tattoo

Helping a stranded driver

Asking someone out on a date

We went through each of these things, and it seemed to take forever. This was really turning into a think-a-thon, and I was getting a headache really bad. I don't always like to think so much, but everything he was saying made a little bit of sense. Dr. Nick could probably tell I was feeling pretty ready to actually start doing something, but I guess he thought now was a good time to tell me what my teacher told him about me.

Dr. Nick said my teacher likes me very much and worries about the risks I take to get noticed by the other kids in class. Dr. Nick said my teacher used the name Daredevil to explain how I always take the dares other kids give me. I've heard my teacher call me that before. That's what all the kids call me too, and I like it! It makes me feel pretty cool, and all the kids know who I am now.

My counselor kept me after the other kids in group went back to their classrooms. Some of the kids were pretty bummed out about losing their lunch, but the counselor surprised each of them with "Eat lunch with the counselor passes." Everybody was pretty happy about that!

The counselor wanted to talk to me about some of the dares the other kids dare me to do. I told him about the time I took the test answer book off the teacher's desk, the time I pulled the fire alarm, and that one time when I walked in front of traffic to make all the cars stop.

When Dr. Nick asked me what the other kids did when I took the book, pulled the alarm, and walked in front of traffic, I told him, "They laughed." The counselor then opened up his dictionary and asked me to look up the word "daredevil." I did. I liked what it said about being brave and admired. He then asked me to look up the word "buffoon." I did. I didn't like what it said about being laughed at and easily tricked by other people.

I was feeling pretty embarrassed, but I felt a lot better when Dr. Nick told me that lots of daredevils start out as buffoons. He also said that learning how to go from buffoon to daredevil depends on how well I figure out what taking chances is all about. He said we could talk about all that stuff during lunch today if I wanted to.

Dear Parent,

"Taking chances" is what many boys and girls haphazardly do. In counseling group today, the students discovered that taking chances always involves the element of risk. Risk being, "things" subject to loss or gain. Today some of those risks included things such as reputation, self esteem, educational status, self image, and safety issues. In helping your child come to better understand "risks," your child also began to better understand the responsibility involved in taking chances.

PRIORITIES

Goal of Activity: To help the student learn to prioritize and accomplish his or her goals within an appropriate amount of time.

Student Mix: boys and girls of similar age and grade

Group Size: four to six students

Suggested Time: twenty to thirty minutes

Materials Required: index cards, party favors, and treats

Considerations:

This is one of my favorite lessons to share with students. It is the anti-excuse activity for girls and boys who chronically make excuses rather than achieve results.

When we help children learn the skills involved in not only prioritizing, but also guide them in how they achieve their priorities, we are really helping them build self-esteem and confidence. To some degree, these are the prerequisites for building successful organizational skills.

Confronting boys and girls about their priorities doesn't always need to be an uncomfortable endeavor. Learning how to state the inferred outcomes of a student's behavior while at the same time being supportive of the student are golden opportunities for the counselor to embrace.

Diplomatic and supportive confrontation is a skill to be learned, not avoided.

Student Reflection:

I knew today was going to be a good day in counseling because I was having a good day. I got up on time, had my backpack ready, homework done, ate breakfast, and left home with my sister on time. When the counselor called my classroom, I was ready to go!

Our group started with Dr. Nick blocking the doorway, and no one could get in unless he gave everyone a treat. This was awesome! Once we had our treat, he let us into his office. He said he really likes that we choose to come to counseling group.

Like always, we said who we are and then got to say things like our age and who our teacher is. One kid thought it would be fun to also say what our favorite book is too. Today was also a day that we talked about some of our goals and stuff. I've been doing pretty well on my goals. I met my reading goal for the year by reading like ten books. I kept my grades all above a B except for a D the teacher gave me in history. I even made my goal of having less than five days being absent for the whole year!

I was a little bit embarrassed in kind of a good way when Dr. Nick threw some little pieces of paper in the air, used a noise maker, and cheered for me after I told him about the goals I met. I felt proud of myself.

After all of our introductions and goals got talked about, we did check-in. Dr. Nick gave each of us a couple minutes to talk about family, school, and friends. Once a kid's two minutes was over, they were done and someone else got to go next.

Two of the girls in our group didn't get done talking in time. Dr. Nick reminded those girls that they had the same amount of time as everyone did. He also told them that it would help them both if they would learn to use their time better.

I think what he said didn't seem to help the girls feel very good. One of the girls got really mad, tipped over a chair, and ran back to her classroom. The other girl stayed in our group but sat there with her head down and arms folded across her chest. I've seen her pout before. I told my friend sitting next to me, "This might mean more candy for us." Dr. Nick used his phone to make sure that one crybaby girl got back to her classroom.

We began our activity with Dr. Nick giving everyone six cards of different colors. Each card had a word written on it. The words were school, play, family, work, friends, and fun. We went over what each word meant and then the counselor wrote the word priority on the whiteboard.

We looked in the dictionary for the word priority and found the definition. Basically, it's like priority means that you put stuff in an order of most important at the top and stuff that's less important gets put after that top one.

Once all the words got figured out, the counselor said we were going to play a special game called T.R.O., which stood for "Time Ran Out." We got the game started with everybody being told to put our word cards in order of being important. Like, I put my highest priority card face down and that would be my first card. Then I put my second most important card next to that one. I did this until all my cards were on the table in my order of importance. I laid them all out in front of me just like the counselor told me and showed me how to do.

When the counselor shouted, "T.R.O.," we had to take our last priority card off the table. Like, when the game first got started, when Dr. Nick called out, "T.R.O." that first time, everyone had to take their sixth priority card off the table and couldn't use it again until the game was over.

After he did that, he asked us what priority card we got rid of. Whenever we did that, he would ask that person some pretty hard questions about why that one was their last priority. Sometimes he would lean way over toward the kids he was questioning and almost get into their faces about their choices!

I know he was just having fun and exaggerating what he was doing, but it sure felt like he was really, really in our business about stuff but in a fun way. The kinds of questions he would ask were things like: "So, play is a greater priority to you than your family?" "Do you think your choice of fun over school has anything to do with your current grades?" "By choosing friends over family, do you understand why your brother might feel like you don't have much time for him?"

This kept happening until all of us were down to only two cards...our first two priorities. Then Dr. Nick called out, "T.R.O." and everyone had to take away their number two priority card from the table.

The counselor then asked what everybody's number one priority card was. Some boys and girls were pretty happy with their first priority card. I was pretty happy with mine, but the girl next to me wasn't! Her first priority card was the play card, and Dr. Nick kinda got all over her about it. He asked Kayla to tell everyone why play is more important to her than family and school. She just got madder and told him, "Because, that's why!" That didn't go over very good.

Dr. Nick settled everybody down and told us there would be days where we may only have a little bit of time to get done only one or two of the things that we need and or wanted to get done. Like, he told me even though I'm pretty good at prioritizing stuff, I might have a day where I have to study for history, do house chores, play video games, and clean up my room.

Next thing I know, the counselor is asking me lots of questions really, really fast. I didn't even have a chance to answer the first question! Here are some of the questions I remember him asking me about my priority choices:

Which one would I do first?

How about second?

Which one would I wait until last to do?

What if I ran out of time and could only get two things done?

What if I ran out of time and only could get one of those things done, which one would it be?

Would I get in trouble if I only got three of those things done?

What would happen if one thing took a lot longer than I thought it would take?

Even though I think I knew the right answers, I was feeling lots of pressure to decide. I felt like my brain was trapped, and my usual answers for not getting history done couldn't get out. Man, was I ever glad when he smiled and told me I didn't have to answer any of his questions! He told me that these are the kind of questions that some kids really need to learn to ask themselves, especially when they have lots of things to do.

While we were sitting at the table, Dr. Nick had us imagine that there are two types of priorities: external and internal. External ones are things outside of our bodies. He said external priorities are things like homework, chores, and other things that we have to get done.

He said internal priorities are things we keep inside our brains and hearts, they tell about stuff we think and feel is important.

Dr. Nick said some examples of internal priorities are things like respecting others, being kind, showing love, being generous, telling the truth, and believing in living life in a good way.

I was kind of getting it but not really understanding for sure what he was talking about. All it took was for me to just look at him with like a big question mark on my face. That's when I push my eyebrows together, scrunch up my nose, and leave my mouth open. It's one of my favorite faces! Dr. Nick said to just think of it all this way, "What you decide to do, what you actually get done, and how you get it done says all you need to know about both kinds of priorities."

The counselor drew a picture of a big fat bag of money on the whiteboard. He told us to pretend that his external priority was to have all that money. He then wrote the words earn, steal, trick, and gamble on the whiteboard.

He pointed to the words he had just written on the whiteboard and said that he could get that money by doing any one of those things like earning, stealing, gambling, or tricking someone to get that money. Then he said how he chooses to go about getting that money would tell us a lot about his internal priorities. Now I got it. That example helped a whole bunch! I guess my question mark face worked again!

Dr. Nick then talked to the girl in our group who had been pouting since check-in. I heard him remind her that she made some choices about how she used her time. I also heard him use his nice voice to encourage her to figure out what her priorities need to be if she wants to be more successful next time.

When the bell rang, Dr. Nick asked everyone to take our priority cards home. He said to use them every day for two weeks and try prioritizing our cards the night before we're supposed to use them the next day. He even thought we should have our parents look them over and help us, just in case we've forgotten anything!

Dr. Nick said it's really a great feeling having our priorities lined up, straightened out, and in the right order to start every day.

Dear Parent,

A group of students including your child participated in a counseling activity game called "Time Ran Out." Not surprisingly, this was a game about learning how to prioritize. Students were given the opportunity to list their favorite things. In a process that led to the elimination of some things due to time restrictions, students discovered the need to re-organize their original list of priorities. For example, after some persuasive discussion, "homework" came to be a greater priority than watching television.

STICKY HANDS

Goal of Activity: To encourage the student to be respectful of other people's property and to promote honest thinking and behavior.

Student Mix: boys and girls of similar age and grade

Group Size: four to six students

Suggested Time: thirty to forty minutes

Materials Required: sticky hands, paper cut-outs, and disposable wash cloths

Considerations:

Every now and then you'll have students who are referred to you for taking things that don't belong to them. By the time you get to see the student, he or she may have already been spoken to by their teacher, principal, and parents multiple times. By now, some of these boys and girls are facing severe consequences for their next violation of stealing. Sometimes, even severe consequences serve only to hinder the determined student from stealing and may, in fact, be interpreted as more of a challenge not to get caught.

For the everyday student in counseling, I think a lesson like this one reinforces what they may already know about how wrong stealing is. There will be occasion, even in the counseling room, when you notice some of the materials you use in activities will turn up missing. It's not uncommon to have students take more than his or her share of candy when offered. Be careful how you go about addressing the subject. Sometimes it's best to gather as much data as you can before you address the issue.

For the student who is developing a chronic and disturbing pattern of theft that borders on clinical interpretation, this lesson may serve as a springboard to a consultation with the school psychologist or a mental health professional outside the school system.

Don't panic, you will learn how and when to make appropriate referrals in time.

Student Reflection:

Dr. Nick came by my room today and took me to be part of counseling group. As we were walking to his office, we stopped by more classrooms looking to get the other kids in our group. Once we all got to his office, he gave everybody one of those little throw away washcloths. He said some of us might have sticky hands so we should get them as clean as possible before he gets our treats out.

One thing was different about check-in, Dr. Nick said we had to use the alphabet to figure out who would go first, second, third, fourth, fifth, and last to talk about school, family, and friends. We voted to use the first letter of our first name to see who would go first.

I noticed during check-in that the counselor asked questions about finding and keeping things. For example, he asked the kid sitting across from me, "Have you ever found something that wasn't yours and kept it?" He asked this one girl if she had ever found something in a library or on the playground and just kept it. Dr. Nick didn't sound mad or anything, just like he wanted to know, that's all. After we all got done with check-in, we started to get ready for the counseling activity.

The counselor gave everybody a sticky hand! The sticky hand was inside a clear plastic wrapper. The hand part was made of some sticky, stretchy, rubbery stuff. At the bottom part of the hand was this long, stretchy rubbery cord used for dangling it or holding on to it like a handle. I don't think any of us were very surprised when Dr. Nick told us the name of the game we were going to play is called "Sticky Hands."

While we were sitting around the table, our counselor laid out a whole bunch of small paper cut-outs. Each cut-out was about the size of the long eraser I keep in my desk next to my new laser pen. It was weird because each cut-out had the name of somebody from our group on it and the name of something on it. Like, one piece of paper had Natalie's name and the word "pencil" on it. Another paper had my name written on it and the word "coin." Dr. Nick told us to notice that every paper had only one person's name written on it along with just one thing like pencil, coin, pen, backpack, bike, ruler, or compass.

I was starting to get pretty excited and really wasn't paying too much attention. I accidentally flung my sticky hand up against the face of the kid sitting next to me. I was glad that Dr. Nick didn't see me do that.

Dr. Nick told us that the purpose of the game is to collect as many cut-out items as possible within a certain amount of time. Players can only collect items with their name on it by dangling the sticky hand into a position that lets the cut-out thing stick to the hand. He said once the hand sticks to the paper, we can take the paper off the hand and place the paper away from the table in our own pile of stuff. A player would automatically lose the game if he or she picked up something with somebody else's name on it. When everyone pretty much knew what to do, Dr. Nick set his timer for sixty seconds. When he said go we could start playing!

Two of the kids in our group did pretty good, another boy threw his sticky hand up against the window, and the girl sitting next to me accidentally took another player's cut-out. She and the boy playing with the window had to stop playing for just that one game.

We played the game a few different times. The only kid who didn't get to play anymore was the boy who kept throwing his sticky hand up against the window. The counselor had that kid go back to his classroom when he hit me in the face with his sticky hand. I got so mad when that kid had hit me in the face, I just wanted to smack him again with my sticky hand! What a creep... he had no reason to do that!

During the game everybody had to keep track of our own things we picked up. When we were done, three kids tied for first place. The counselor said everyone did a great job of being careful and picking up just the stuff they were supposed to.

After we finished playing, we talked about the game. Dr. Nick told us that our game had goals, rules, and consequences for not playing the right way. He said the goal of the game was to have fun and win. The rules of the game had players collecting only their own things in a certain amount of time. The game also had consequences for breaking the rules. The consequence for break-ing any of the rules was not being able to play anymore.

Dr. Nick cleared the table of all its stuff and told us he would give back the sticky hands after group for us to keep. He said he wanted to talk about how our game was really a game about learning not to take things that don't belong to us. He said that the "Sticky Hands" game should really be called the "Don't Steal" game! Our counselor told us to think about some of the ques-tions he asked us during check-in, like finding and keeping things that don't belong to us.

We talked about some of the consequences of taking things

that are better left alone. Some of the consequences Dr. Nick wrote on the whiteboard were physical punishments like spanking, loss of privileges like free time, restrictions to our room, and more chores to do at home.

Consequences of stealing stuff at school could turn into detentions or suspensions and would probably make other kids and teachers think of us as being a stealer. Stealing from a friend could really be bad! Who wants a friend you can't trust? Who is going to invite a stealer over to his house? No one at school is going to hang out with a kid who's a stealer! As soon as I thought about all that stuff about stealing, I remembered the laser light I found lost in this kid's desk from my room. What should I do now?

Dr. Nick said he wanted us to talk to each other about how we've felt when we've had our own stuff stolen from our desks, houses, and yards. He also wrote down some words on the whiteboard that we could use. Words like, angry, betrayed, cheated, ripped off, hurt, and confused.

After we had talked for a few minutes, the counselor said something like how temptation or wanting to take something that's not yours, can cause sticky hands. He also said that it's important to be respectful of other people's property, such as pencils, pens, coins, and toys, no matter how much temptation we feel. I liked that Dr. Nick said to think of some temptations as being like bad dares. Like, even though it might take a lot of courage to take something, it takes a lot more of a better courage to give it back.

When me and the other kids left counseling group, Dr. Nick gave all of us three or four more little packages of those throw away washcloths. He said we should have them just in case we ever feel like temptation is giving us sticky hands.

I think I know what to do now.

Dear Parent,

Kids sometimes take things that don't belong to them, either intentionally or unintentionally. The counseling lesson today addressed both concerns. In a game called "Sticky Hands," students were given permission to pick up paper cut-out items with only their name on them. The game had a goal, rules, and consequences. There are also goals, rules, and consequences in the home and at school regarding "picking up" things without permission. Be sure to check out your child's "Sticky Hand."

IN OUR ABSENCE

Goal of Activity: To encourage the student to do his or her best in the absence of guiding eyes.

Student Mix: individualized

Group Size: individualized

Suggested Time: individualized

Materials Required: letter and handout

Considerations:

I've had opportunity to use this activity several times over the course of the past few years with a dual purpose in mind. The activity, on one level, provides the student with a reminder of how behavior not only affects reputation but also reflects character. The lesson also provides boys and girls with an opportunity to think about doing their best in all they say and do, even if no one is looking. That is, in the absence of counselors, coaches, principals, parents, or other guiding figures, the expectation for the student to do his or her best with family, school, and friends is still present. For counselors, helping boys and girls learn how to guide and conduct themselves appropriately throughout the course of their lives, is often the underlying and unwritten goal every counselor has for the students on their case load.

Understandably, planning our own absence is a worthwhile lesson for boys and girls to learn how to deal with. For some students, this may be one of the first of many lifelong opportunities they are given in hopes of learning the benefits of this valuable lesson. When their classroom teacher is absent, for example, students are expected to continue do their best and behave well for the substitute teacher. For counselors, however, the counseling substitute becomes the combined account of memories and experiences the student has incorporated in his or her life through the activities and lessons you, the counselor, have provided.

Student Reflection:

Me and my friend ran over to Dr. Nick's office at recess today to see if he was here. Mrs. Carly the speech lady told us she hadn't seen him yet. I wasn't the only one there either, there were like five other kids looking for him too! When I got back to my classroom, I just sat there looking at the clock and waiting for the phone to ring.

I had to get out my math stuff and that's when the phone rang! I hurried up and was just about out the door, but my teacher called me back to the classroom. She told me that Dr. Nick was not here today. That meant no group. I was so bummed out and disappointed!

Just about before lunch time, my teacher put an envelope on my desk and asked me to open it. The letter was from Dr. Nick! He had written me like an apology letter! The apology was for not being able to be in counseling group today. He wrote that even though he likes me a ton and has fun being with me in group, there might be some days when he's not able to be around but to still do my best. Today is one of those days.

In his letter, Dr. Nick said he wanted me to be thinking about my family, school, and my friends even if I wasn't in group. He wrote that everybody in counseling group did a great job in learn-ing lots since we've been in counseling this year. He wanted me to remember all the time our group had spent talking about the important people in our lives and how much those people mean to us.

In the letter, Dr. Nick said, "Counseling works best on focused and alert minds. Like, counseling is sort of like a ride at Great America, you walk in, sit down, buckle up, hold on, and keep your eyes and ears wide open." That's for sure! I remember lots of times when counseling group was just like that!

Dr. Nick wrote that some kids might start counseling with the attitude of just going along for the ride, but once a kid really starts getting into counseling, they start using some of the stuff they've learned from group with their family, school, and friends. He said it's like once I realize I'm using some of the things I've learned in group with other people, that's when I know what counseling is all about!

He wrote down that realizing what counseling is all about might be like when I get in the car with my family to drive home from the theme park. As soon as I sit down and get my seatbelt on, I might remember seeing the picture of me on the roller coaster that I saw when I was leaving the ride area. That's when I'll remember I'm really buckling up with my family and friends for the real ride!

In that letter, Dr. Nick wrote I should try to remember as many of our counseling activities as I could think of. Like which ones I liked and which ones I didn't like so much. For sure, he wants me to think about and remember what the activities were really about and how I could use that stuff when I'm with my family, teachers, and friends.

Even though we didn't have group today, Dr. Nick had stapled a counseling activity sheet on my letter for me to do. The activity is supposed to help me figure out not only what my name means, but what it would mean to people who don't know me so good like he does.

The instructions he wrote were about how to translate what my name means. He wrote that one of the best ways to figure out who somebody is would be by watching what and how that person does their stuff. Like, Dr. Nick knows our names because of how we act and what we're trying to do. He says he sees tons of good things in us, especially me! For sure he wants other people to see me the same way he does, but he knows that other people may only get to know me by listening to what I say and watching what I do.

Dr. Nick wrote that the activity sheet gives me the chance to better figure out who I am and how I should act around other people. He thinks it's also going to help other people think of me the way he does. He wrote that maybe I could get the help of my teacher and mom or dad to go through the list of words with me because they might see things in me or know things about me that I don't. That's for sure! I don't even know what some of these words mean!

At the bottom of his letter, Dr. Nick wrote with a red marker that I should be keeping my name code in a place like on my refrigerator or in my backpack so I'll always remember who I am and which words should be guiding what I say and do.

WHAT MY NAME SAYS ABOUT ME!

* Write your first name from top along the left side of the paper (one letter for each space.)

* Using the behavior letter/work code, assign each letter of your name a coinciding word that describes the type of person you are.

* From those words, circle the words that describe you most of the time and underline the words that describe you some of the time.

_____ _____

_____ _____

_____ _____

_____ _____

_____ _____

_____ _____

_____ _____

_____ _____

_____ _____

_____ _____

_____ _____

A=Understanding   H=Trustworthy   O=Faithful   V=Strong
B=Caring   I=Honest   P=Giving   W=Patient
C=Sharing   J=Compassionate   Q=Special   X=Loyal
D=Dependable   K=Thougthful   R=Respectful   Y=Positive
E=Reliable   L=Thankful   S=Responsible   Z=Nice
F=Sincere   M=Kind   T=Courteous
G=Fun   N=Supportive   U=Affectionate

Dear Parent,

Today's counseling activity was very different from the activities your child usually participates in. The counselor was absent! In the counselor's absence, however, students were delivered an activity sheet designed to help them better understand who they are and how they need to be behaving if they intend to be successful. In a letter from the counselor, students were encouraged to do their best in everything they say and do regardless of the absence of significant others throughout their lives.

"WE COME TO NEW BEGINNINGS ONLY AT THE END"

~ William Bridges

ABOUT THE AUTHOR

Nicholas George Minardi was born and raised in Omaha, Nebraska. He attended and received his Bachelors degree from Dakota Wesleyan University in Mitchell, S.D. From there he moved to Aberdeen, S.D. and completed his Masters degree in Guidance & Counseling from Northern State University. Having moved to California, he earned his Ph.D. from Rosebridge Graduate School and later, his license to practice Clinical Psychology. Dr. Nick continues to enjoy his work as a school counselor.

For more information and downloads, please visit:

fiftystepscloser.com